The Absolute and Star Trek

George A. Gonzalez

The Absolute and Star Trek

George A. Gonzalez
Department of Political Science
University of Miami
Coral Gables, Florida, USA

ISBN 978-3-319-47793-0   ISBN 978-3-319-47794-7 (eBook)
DOI 10.1007/978-3-319-47794-7

Library of Congress Control Number: 2016957406

Cover illustration: Mono Circles © John Rawsterne/patternhead.com

Printed on acid-free paper

This Palgrave Macmillan imprint is published by Springer Nature
The registered company is Springer International Publishing AG
The registered company address is: Gewerbestrasse 11, 6330 Cham, Switzerland

For Ileana and Alana

PREFACE

How can we know the *Absolute?*—through art.[1] The *absolute*, philosophized upon most saliently by Georg Hegel,[2] is the driving force behind history.[3] Classicist Henry Paolucci explains that "art" (along with religion and philosophy) "are in the end, for Hegel, 'moments' of *absolute spirit.*"[4] Similarly, philosopher William Desmond, in *A Study of Hegel's Aesthetics: Art and the Absolute*, notes that "Art has an *absolute* dimension; indeed, it belongs together with religion and philosophy itself as one of the three highest modes of human meaning."[5] Consonant with Hegelian reasoning, my specific argument in this volume is that the broadcast iterations of Star Trek allow us to comprehend significant aspects of the absolute. Therefore, Star Trek is the highest of highbrow entertainment.[6]

Why is art an empirical documentation of the *absolute?*[7] Humans speculate about the absolute—i.e., that which moves history forward and allows people to lead authentic lives. Precisely because the *absolute* is that which is and which isn't,[8] art/imagination allows for the *absolute* to be conveyed in an intellectually and emotionally satisfying matter.[9] (Notably, the first known philosophy in the Western world [Plato's *Dialogues*] was written in the form of narrative art.) Art, therefore, can supersede philosophy, with the latter serving to dissect/amplify what is accessed/depicted through the former.

A simple but nonetheless informative example being the *Star Trek: The Next Generation* (1987–1994) episode "All Goods Things..." (1994). The "little pond of goo" from which all life on Earth emanated is conveyed in the following figure. It is from this *pond of goo* that the *absolute* for organic life on Earth was born, as here is where the will (i.e., *spirit*) to

Fig. 1 "Everything you know, your entire civilization, it all begins right here in this little pond of goo"

live/survive/procreate on this planet was spawned. Star Trek aptly notes that the destruction of this pond, and all like it, would have prevented humans from evolving. It is through such portrayals that we can *see* how the absolute operates with regard to life on Earth (of course, including humans).

The enduring popularity of the Star Trek franchise indicates the validity of the speculation portrayed in the franchise about the absolute. Put differently, the global success of the Star Trek franchise validates the idea that the multiple series and movies, to an important degree, "capture" the essence of the absolute. Philosophy Professor Jack Kaminsky, drawing explicitly on Hegel's theory of aesthetics, explains that "the artist tries to show men what kind of man would be the fullest expression of the Idea" (i.e., the *Absolute*).[10] Therefore, very plausibly, the artistic success of the Star Trek franchise (and its great popularity) is precisely due to the fact that it shows us *what kind of person/society would be the fullest expression of the Absolute*. Precisely because of Star Trek we can seemingly be secure about certain aspects of the absolute, and, as a result, Star Trek ostensibly serves as a guide to an authentic life and a stable, thriving society. Parenthetically, the value of

Star Trek is exactly that it transcends the personalities and specific contexts within which it was produced. Indeed, this is precisely what makes it effective, elucidating political theory and philosophy.

Analytic philosophy, whose adherents have historically ridiculed the idea of the absolute[11]—without positing any answers of their own for the movement of history[12]—is an obstacle to knowledge. Most specifically, art and the analyzing of the aesthetic are viewed by analytic philosophers as mainly outside of epistemology and ignorable as it relates to science.[13] Instead, the humanities is of a piece with the physical sciences[14]—as they both *speculate* about the absolute, the latter about its manifestation in matter and energy, whereas the former (in its finer forms) is *speculation* about the absolute as it pertains to human affairs.[15] "Art may not have the precision of physics but, according to Hegel, it has as crucial a role in revealing to us an aspect of the [Absolute] Idea."[16] Because analytic philosophers reject the arts as a source of knowledge, this approach serves to block the truth—knowledge of the absolute through art (Chapter 2). Taking the argument further, Star Trek indicates that the purpose of humanity is precisely to *speculate* about the world/universe through both science and the humanities (Chapter 3).

CONTENTS

LIST OF FIGURES

CHAPTER 1

Introduction

Abstract This volume treats the metaphysics of the broadcast iterations of Star Trek. This is my second book on the Star Trek franchise. The first, titled *The Politics of Star Trek*, explored the political theory underlying the Star Trek phenomenon. Here, I more directly focus on issues associated with the field of metaphysics: what is an *authentic* life; similarly, what is the purpose of life; what is knowledge (epistemology); and how hewing to an unauthentic life, negating the purpose of life, as well as how ignoring actual knowledge leads to disaster for humanity/civilization. I will show in this volume (as I did in my first Star Trek book) that this franchise is key to understanding the prime issues that confront humanity in the twenty-first century.

Keywords Georg Hegel · The Absolute · Star Trek

This volume treats the metaphysics of the broadcast iterations of Star Trek. This is my second book on the Star Trek franchise. The first, titled *The Politics of Star Trek*, explored the political theory underlying the Star Trek phenomenon.[17] Here, I more directly focus on issues associated with the field of metaphysics: what is an *authentic* life; similarly, what is the purpose of life; what is knowledge (epistemology); and how hewing to an unauthentic life, negating the purpose of life, as well as how ignoring actual knowledge leads to disaster for humanity/civilization. I will show in this volume

© The Author(s) 2017

G.A. Gonzalez, *The Absolute and Star Trek*,

DOI 10.1007/978-3-319-47794-7_1

1

(as I did in my first Star Trek book) that this franchise is key to understanding the prime issues that confront humanity in the twenty-first century.

The political theory core of *The Politics of Star Trek* is *Marxism* and *pragmatism/neopragmatism*. As I argue that these are at the center of the Star Trek text. Importantly, Karl Marx[18] and the Marxist revolutionary Leon Trotsky[19] are directly referred to in the text. Thus, at least some of the creators of this text were consciously aware of the parallel between the sweep of the franchise (at least up until *Star Trek: Enterprise* [2001–2005]) and the politics inspired by Marx and Trotsky. Beginning with *Star Trek* (1966–1969) the original series, the Star Trek franchise is marked with a thorough exposition and critique of *pragmatism* and *neo-pragmatism* (*inter-subjective agreement*)—holding that pragmatism and neo-pragmatism are the basis of slavery, torture, authoritarianism, and the ultimate destruction of civilization/humanity. With the 1996 movie *First Contact*, and the series *Enterprise*, the political theory of the franchise shifts to the ideation of Carl Schmitt—with Schmitt-like thinking expressly used.[20]

What the creators of Star Trek may be less aware of is how their text reflects Hegelian reasoning. Given that most of Star Trek is founded directly upon Marxism, it should not be surprising that a strong relationship exists between Star Trek and Georg Hegel's philosophy. It is broadly understood that Marx viewed much of his work as an improvement on Hegel's ideas.[21] In drawing on Hegel, I show that Star Trek can be used as a corrective to Marx—or least the broad perception of him. Marx's major contribution to Western philosophy is his materialist understanding of society. In developing his theories Marx was consciously remedying what he saw as the undue emphasis on idealism by Hegel. Thus, while Marx never denied the importance of ideas to the development of society, his prime focus was on the development of the means of production to analyze the social/political evolution of society.

Star Trek in no way suggests that Marx is wrong in linking the politics of a society to its means of production. Nevertheless, Star Trek does stress modes of thought (idealism) in the forward movement of the *progressive dialectic*—explicitly identified by Marx, acted upon by Trotsky, and artistically conveyed in Star Trek (as shown in *The Politics of Star Trek*). Importantly, Star Trek does not indicate (*á la* utopian socialists) that all we have to do is argue effectively for a socialist society. Instead, Star Trek posits people must possess the correct attitudes in order to bring about an ideal socialist society: (1) a commitment to social justice; (2) an unyielding commitment to the truth; and (3) a similar commitment to scientific, intellectual discovery. The embracing of these outlooks (frames of thought) is the only way that people can "see" the *absolute* and bring it fully to fruition (*á la* the progressive dialectic) (Chapter 4).

Therefore, what Star Trek brings to the fore of Marxist reasoning is the fact that the harmonious/thriving socialist/communist society envisioned by Marx may not come to fruition. This is because people may not develop the correct attitude toward the *absolute*. If so, the end result is societal collapse and seemingly a nightmare scenario/dystopia for humanity. Thus, one broad critique that could be made of Marx is that he is seemingly too sanguine about the transition to socialism following the collapse of capitalism resulting from its inherent "contradictions."[22] Hence, it is left for Rosa Luxemburg to opine that the future is either "socialism or barbarism."[23] Star Trek takes this warning seriously, and explicitly argues that the correct type of "attitude" and, presumably, leadership are needed for a successful transition from capitalism to a thriving/sustainable socialism. Without these, *barbarism* may very well be the outcome of the collapse of capitalism.

Hegel and Star Trek also conjecture on the outlooks that can lead us away from the *absolute* and astray from the *progressive dialectic*. Hegel wrote of "bad infinities,"[24] or ideas that prevent us from seeing the absolute and fulfilling its promise. Drawing on the experiences and philosophies of the twentieth and twenty-first centuries, Star Trek identifies four *false infinities*— or false dawns, siren songs (if I may)—that could lead humanity to disaster: (1) *traditionalism* (*pre-modernism*); (2) *Nazism*; (3) Schmitt's *friend/foe* dichotomy; and (4) *neoliberal capitalism* (Chapters 4 through 7). Moreover, precisely because *pragmatism* and *neo-pragmatism* prioritize societal stability over ethics and justice, they, too, are false infinities (Chapter 8). In Chapter 9, I argue that one factor that makes zombies and the Borg such frightening (fictional) threats is that their total victory would mean the end of *speculation* and the quest for "Absolute Knowledge." Star Trek does more than draw out and specify Hegel's warning on *false infinites*. Star Trek demonstrates the triumph of Hegel's *speculative* reasoning over analytic philosophy. At the heart of Hegel's philosophy (and Star Trek) is speculation about *The Absolute* and how to bring it to fruition. Therefore, Star Trek, as arguably the most popular television franchise in all of history, demonstrates that people are not very concerned about the "fear of error" (i.e., analytic philosophy) and instead place ultimate value on speculation—about justice, truth, knowledge, an authentic life, etc. In Chapter 2, I take up a treatment of Star Trek based on the "fear of error"—again, analytic philosophy.

OVERVIEW OF BOOK

Chapters 2 and 3 are focused on how Star Trek is fundamentally a text about the Hegelian absolute, with the text making both indirect and direct references to the absolute. Therefore, a treatment of the Star Trek franchise motivated by analytic philosophy vacates/elides its normative/philosophical core (Chapter 2). Chapter 3 outlines how the Star Trek text is based on speculation of the *absolute*. Chapter 4: *The Absolute* is manifest in Star Trek as a progressive dialectic, where through revolutionary stages/events humanity overcomes neoliberalism as well as capitalism to establish a classless society—free of gender and ethnic biases. Chapters 5 through 7 analyze *false infinities* (or undesirable societal outcomes) as cast in Star Trek. False infinities represent instances where societies turn away from the Absolute and the progressive dialectic, which leads to societal dysfunction, instability, and potentially the destruction of civilization. Judging from Star Trek, the philosophers of Friedrich Nietzsche, Martin Heidegger, Carl Schmitt, and Leo Strauss all proffer false infinities (Chapter 5). Chapters 6 and 7 treat false infinities that inhere in Heidegger's notion of "Dasein." Heidegger rejects the universalism of the Hegelian absolute, and instead holds that language, prejudices, culture (i.e., Dasein) serve as the legitimate basis of society. As already noted, Chapter 8 analyzes the false infinities of pragmatism and neo-pragmatism as outlined Star Trek, and Chapter 9 compares zombies and the Borg and how they represent fictional threats to the quest for Absolute Knowledge.

CHAPTER 2

Analytic Philosophy and Star Trek

Abstract Hegel's *absolute* is embedded in the Star Trek text. This is clearly evident in the episode "Transfiguration"—with a character achieving knowledge of the *whole*. "Sacred Ground" explicitly points to "spirits"—in the Hegelian sense—and the idea that *the real* extends beyond the material, so-called rational, realm. More than just postulating the existence of the absolute, Star Trek ostensibly makes the argument that through honesty, selflessness, and a commitment to scientific, intellectual discovery people can know the absolute and bring forth its promise.

Keywords Georg Hegel · Analytic Philosophy · The Absolute · Star Trek

Philosopher Richard Hanley wrote *The Metaphysics of Star Trek*. Hanley describes himself as an analytic (or Anglo-American) philosopher. Hanley adds that he considers himself a proponent of "*naturalism*—roughly, the view that philosophy is and ought to be continuous with the natural sciences, since both enterprises employ the combination of reason and empirical investigation."[25] Why would a philosopher who considers his research an adjunct to the natural sciences undertake an analysis of a fictional television series? Hanley indicates he has undertaken his book as "a useful introduction to the contemporary debates concerning humankind's place in the world."[26] Again, why is Star Trek a useful venue for this purpose? Hanley never explains.

Whether Hanley intends it or not, his book can be grouped with a virtual genre within *Star Trek Studies* that adopts a hostile and captious attitude toward the franchise.[27] In *The Politics of Star Trek* I take up the claims against the franchise of its being pro-American, racist, and pro-imperialist. While Star Trek does replicate the clash of civilization idea,[28] the franchise is, nevertheless, progressive, internationalist, fair-minded, and anti-imperialist.

While Hanley avoids incendiary and slanderous aspersions, he does don a gratuitously critical attitude toward Star Trek. He makes picayune or nitpick quips about the Star Trek text. For instance, Hanley takes issue with the fact that Data, an android, is cast as capable of ingesting/processing food; being inebriated through the consumption of alcohol; and engaging in sex.[29] Hanley's tack in analyzing Star Trek acts as something of a killjoy—with Hanley acknowledging at one point that his treatment is boring.[30] Thus, Hanley's goal in his book is not to engage readers in the Star Trek text, but quite the opposite—to pierce the imaginative bubble that surrounds a popular franchise character (Data), and, generally, to throw cold water on plot devices used in the franchise (for example, time travel). How does such an attitude toward a work of fiction forward the natural sciences? Does Hanley actually fear that scientists will mistake Data for a person or make an error in viewing him as a non-person? Will people wrongly believe that time travel is possible from watching Star Trek?

This is not to suggest that Star Trek's artistic choices in relation to science are beyond critique. I, myself, point out that the franchise's use of what it calls "dilithium crystals" serves to elide difficult questions—scarcity, pollution, global warming—with regard to energy. Star Trek, in this instance, is inappropriately optimistic and draws on fantasy to avoid profound issues facing modernity and humanity, more broadly.[31]

I do not see how Hanley's analytic philosophy aids the natural sciences. His attitude amounts to little more than arguing that this or that is beyond our scientific means.[32] If people actually looked to analytic philosophy for guidance, they would be demoralized and dissuaded from trying to improve upon our manipulation of the laws of physics. Thus, to argue that Data (in reality) couldn't do this or that, or holding that time travel is outside the realm of possibility, is to stifle the kind of dreaming and imagining necessary for the advancement of science.

With regard to my critique of Star Trek's dilithium crystals, they are not cast as an invention of the human mind, but a product of nature—something that has no basis in our understanding of the natural world. Thus, while humans may some day invent the equivalent of dilithium crystals, there is no reason to think that nature anywhere has "created" them—as held in Star Trek.

While Hanley's book can be looked upon as playful scholasticism, I hold it has definite political implications. In *The Politics of Star Trek* I make the following observation:

> The Star Trek franchise taps into the prime philosophical dilemma in modern society: striving for justice (*liberal humanism*) or settling for stability (*pragmatism* and *neo-pragmatism*). Thus, judging from Star Trek, the modern mind (the American Mind[?]) sees that modernity can be used to establish a global regime of justice. The fear, however, is that such visions are utopian (i.e., unattainable) and/or implementing such a vision is risky insofar as an effort to revolutionize (profoundly reform) society could result in anarchy (i.e., societal/political breakdown). Reflective of these fears, within modes of thought rooted in *pragmatism* and *neopragmatism* is the idea that the best humanity can hope for is stability (i.e., sufficient *intersubjective agreement*) and should eschew universal concepts of justice.[33]

Thus, in sowing unnecessary doubts in the Star Trek text, Hanley is heightening anxieties about the feasibility of the type of social change depicted in this text.

This charge could be made of analytic philosophy *writ large*. The height of dominance of analytic philosophy in American academia coincides with the post–World War II period,[34] when New Deal state-managerialism[35] and Soviet "socialism" were in political ascendency—and people were hoping for/expecting further government involvement in regulating/replacing the free market.[36] Moreover, during the 1960s, as the Civil Rights Movement, *Star Trek*, and the student movements were communicating the public's aspirations for major, progressive social/political change, American philosophers were mostly bound up with an intellectual project of professional naysaying.[37]

Science and Star Trek

In considering whether or not analytic philosophy is actually useful to the physical sciences, I would submit that narratives like Star Trek are more valuable to the sciences than the captious tack of the analytic philosopher. Star Trek is not solely a work of technological optimism—i.e., the idea that technological advancement will alone drive social/political progress.[38] In fact,

Star Trek renders cautions against unchecked/unregulated scientific/technological advancement.[39] One theme that appears in the Star Trek franchise is eugenics. In Star Trek's histiography in the Earth's past (or our near future) there is a *Eugenics War*—"an improved breed of human. That's what the Eugenics War was all about." The war resulted when "young supermen" seized "power simultaneously in over forty nations... They were aggressive, arrogant. They began to battle among themselves."[40] As a result of this experience, human genetic engineering is banned in the fictional world of Star Trek (e.g., "Doctor Bashir, I Presume?" 1997—*Deep Space Nine*). The other prime caution that Star Trek yields against "technologism" (i.e., an uncritical faith in science/engineering) is the Borg. The Borg (first appearing in *The Next Generation*) embraces technology to such an extreme extent that they replace large parts of their body (and brain) with gadgets. (Every Borg is mechanically altered—by force if necessary.) The result is the Borg do not create knowledge but can only appropriate (i.e., "assimilate") it from others.[41] Hence, a prominent argument in Star Trek is that if technological development is to serve as a basis for justice, freedom, and societal well-being, humanity must get its politics "right"—otherwise technological/scientific advancement can result in eugenics, for instance, or other inherently oppressive/destructive outcomes (e.g., the Borg). Therefore, Star Trek helps us to cogitate about which technologies/advancements to pursue (or not) and how to apply them (or not).[42]

Conversely, Hanley's treatment of Star Trek offers little to no guidance for the sciences, including the psychological sciences. For instance, referencing an episode where Captain Kirk is spilt into two people—one representing his reasoning faculties and the other his emotions—Hanley delves into a discussion on the human "mind." He explains that human personality and desires are driven by a combination of emotion and reason. Hanley holds that pondering the ideal mix of emotion and reason in decision-making will not guide us toward any particular goal. Therefore, according to Hanley, his musings can apply to a selfless healer or a serial killer.[43] As explained in the next section, Star Trek does suggest why a good emotion/reason balance is important: to know the *absolute*.

EMOTION AND REASON IN STAR TREK

Star Trek indicates that those with a good reason/emotion equilibrium can most readily perceive the *absolute*, and act on its knowledge and be motivated by its justice.[44] Both Captains Kirk and Picard (for instance) are paragons of the proper admixture of emotion and reason. Broadly speaking, Star Trek is optimistic insofar as arguing that as global society accepts modernity; reason; science (i.e., the Enlightenment) humans will collectively achieve a higher plane of intelligence; knowledge; and emotional maturity. While Data declares on numerous occasions that he lacks emotion, he does act on the desire (an emotion) to complete missions, to carry out orders, protect the innocent, etc. It would appear that the success of the character Data (artistically speaking) is in significant part derived from his being written with the appropriate balance between reason and emotion.

Moreover, in "Transfigurations" (1990—*Next Generation*), Star Trek makes the explicit argument that those with the appropriate zen can see and possibly even become the absolute. "John Doe," as he regains his memories and bearings, is finally able to transform into seemingly the *whole*—the absolute. (John: "my species is on the verge of a wondrous evolutionary change. A transmutation beyond our physical being. I am the first of my kind to approach this metamorphosis." "My people are about to embark upon a new realm, a new plane of existence." [See Figs. 2.1, 2.2, and 2.3].) The character is cast as possessing a quality of peace and kindness. (Enterprise's Dr. Crusher to John: "I don't believe you're capable of harming any[one]."

In contrast to John Doe, who seemingly achieves the ideal balance between emotion and reason (or zen) and ostensibly comes to completely know (perhaps become) the absolute, Commander Sunad of Zalkon—who demands John be killed—is dominated by "fear" of social change. ("The Zalkonians are afraid of John.") They are fearful that John's transformation is subversive. Sunad charges that John "is a disruptive influence. He spreads lies. He encourages dissent. He disturbs the natural order of our society." (John: Zalkon's "leaders . . . claimed we were dangerous so they destroyed anyone who exhibited the signs of the transfiguration.")

Sunad's fear prevents him from embracing the fact that John has achieved a higher plane of existence, and when John offers him the knowledge of this existence ("Let me show you") Sunad rejects it ("Don't touch me!"). Sunad "feels personally threatened by John." Thus, Sunad's instrumental reason[45] (i.e., his desire for political authority; high social status; and social/political stability as an end unto itself) prevents him from literally seeing/knowing the absolute.

While "Transfigurations" suggests the existence of the absolute, the *Star Trek: Voyager* (1995–2001) episode "Sacred Ground" (1996) makes direct reference to the existence of "spirits"—a term Hegel himself would

Fig. 2.1   John Doe prior to his transformation

Fig. 2.2   John Doe after his transformation

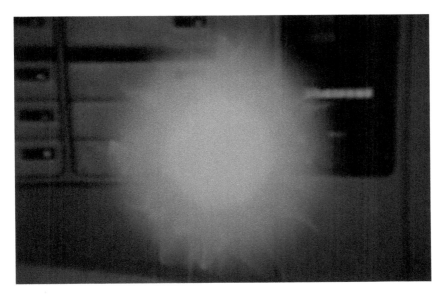

Fig. 2.3 John Doe presumably as knowledge of the *whole*

use to denote something beyond material existence. During the episode, the following is said to Janeway: "Mathematics. I can see why you enjoyed it. Solve a problem, get an answer. The answer is either right or wrong. It's very *absolute*." A veiled reference to Hegel's philosophy? Indicative of Hegelian reasoning the following point is made: "Real is such a relative term." Janeway's materialist (i.e., analytic philosophy) thinking is described in the following: "That would be nice and quantifiable for you, wouldn't it. If the spirits were something you could see and touch and scan with your little devices." Overtly critiquing Kantian rationalism,[46] the following is said to Janeway: "There you go again, always looking for a rational explanation. Well there isn't one."

The action of "Sacred Ground" centers on the fact that Kes (a member of the Voyager crew) becomes incapacitated when she comes into contact with an "energy field" (see Fig. 2.4). Voyager's doctor is unable to bring Kes out of her coma and she is on the verge of death. Unable to find a scientific explanation for the field or Kes's condition, Captain Janeway is forced to appeal to the "monks" that oversee the energy field. They consider it a manifestation of their deities—the *Ancestral Spirits*. In order to save Kes, Janeway is told "that the only

Fig. 2.4   Kes peering at the "Ancestral Spirits"

thing that matters is finding your connection to the spirits."[47] In the end, it is only when Janeway accepts that something beyond material reality exists (i.e., the *Ancestral Spirits*) that Kes is revived.

Star Trek indicates that the zen required to know the absolute is achieved through honesty, selflessness, and a commitment to intellectual, scientific discovery/knowledge. These are the values at the core of the *Federation*. Captain Picard declares that "The first duty of every Starfleet officer is to the *truth*. Whether it's scientific truth, or historical truth, or personal truth. *It is the guiding principle upon which Starfleet is based*" ("The First Duty" 1992—*Next Generation*).[48] (Starfleet is the military institution of the Federation.) Indicating the selfless politics and economics of twenty-third-century humanity, Captain Kirk explains to someone in early twentieth century that "*Let me help*" "A hundred years or so from now ... a famous novelist will write a classic using that theme. He'll recommend those three words even over *I love you*" ("City on the Edge of Forever" 1967—original series). In making the case for a federated interstellar political system to an audience of delegates of the would-be *United Federation of Planets*,

Captain Archer emphasizes the overriding importance of space exploration and expanding scientific knowledge:

> Up until about a hundred years ago, there was one question that burned in every human, that made us study the stars and dream of traveling to them, Are we alone? Our generation is privileged to know the answer to that question. We are all explorers, driven to know what's over the horizon, what's beyond our own shores. And yet, the more I've experienced, the more I've learned that no matter how far we travel, or how fast we get there, the most profound discoveries are not necessarily beyond that next star. They're within us, woven into the threads that bind us, all of us, to each other. The final frontier begins in this hall. Let's explore it together. ("Terra Prime" 2005—*Enterprise*)

According to Star Trek, (as described in Chapter 4) a society founded upon honesty, selflessness, and intellectual, scientific discovery/knowledge comes about through the rejection of capitalism and the replacement of the neo-liberal world order. Thus, only through the rejection of instrumental reason (see Chapter 8) as a philosophical/political foundation can a society achieve the absolute.

CONCLUSION

Star Trek is a work of science fiction. Hanley's analytic philosophy takes the science part too seriously, thereby adopting a captious tack toward the Star Trek franchise. It is the fiction side of the franchise that matters. Through artistic choices, Star Trek's creators intelligently explore the political and social issues that confront humanity in the modern era. Despite Hanley's careful attention to the Star Trek text, this is lost to him.

In confronting these issues, as I noted in *The Politics of Star Trek*, the makers of the franchise draw on Marxism, and posit key critiques of *pragmatism/neo-pragmatism*. Perhaps by happenstance (more likely not), Star Trek also points to Georg Hegel's reasoning and normative approach. Hegel's *absolute* is embedded in the Star Trek text. This is clearly evident in the episode "Transfiguration"—with a character achieving knowledge of the *whole*. "Sacred Ground" explicitly points to "spirits"—in the Hegelian sense—and the idea that *the real* extends beyond the material, so-called rational, realm. More than just postulating the existence of the absolute, Star Trek ostensibly makes the argument that through honesty, selflessness, and a commitment to scientific, intellectual discovery people can know the absolute and bring forth its promise.

As I show beginning with Chapter 4, Star Trek just does not only offer a path to personal enlightenment/knowledge. Instead, the franchise makes the argument that society as whole must move toward the absolute if humanity is to thrive and excel. Society moves toward the absolute through the *progressive dialectic*—again, outlined in Chapter 4.

Next, I show that speculation is at the heart of the Star Trek franchise. Conversely, the franchise rejects analytic philosophy and its "fear of error."

CHAPTER 3

Speculation in Star Trek

Abstract While speculation is deemed central to humanity's evolutionary process and humans' authenticity, Star Trek makes the argument that the absolute operates as a progressive dialectic. Therefore, when we speculate and garner knowledge we are fulfilling the promise of the absolute, which is rational and leading humanity toward a classless society, free of gender/ethnic biases. We speculate and achieve this knowledge in spite of the risk of death. Therefore, analytic philosophy, and its fear of error, is misplaced because humans existentially fear lack of knowledge of the absolute more than they fear error and the death that can result from error.

Keywords Georg Hegel · The Absolute · Star Trek

Whether Data can be deemed a "person" in a scientific sense is—as I already indicated—irrelevant. The fact, however, that viewers seemingly accept Data as a person is significant. Artistically speaking, Data is a *person* because he's able to *speculate*, and not simply simulate speculation (i.e., the Turing Test). In "The Measure of a Man" (1989—*Next Generation*) it is established that Data is "self-aware." Hence, Data knows he is conscious (i.e., "I think, therefore, I am"), and can speculate on his consciousness (i.e., its abilities; purpose; social role, etc.)—consciousness *for-itself.*

© The Author(s) 2017
G.A. Gonzalez, *The Absolute and Star Trek*,
DOI 10.1007/978-3-319-47794-7_3

In the episode "Where Silence has Lease" (1988—*Next Generation*), when the Enterprise is initially trapped in a void, Captain Picard asks Data to "speculate" about it. He then proceeds to do so—sparking a metaphysical discussion with a crew member that Picard shuts down because the gravity of the moment precludes a purely abstract discussion. With this ability to speculate, Data makes meaningful contributions to scientific knowledge—that is, forwarding our understanding of the *absolute*. The character as written speculates with a complete commitment to objectivity, truth, and loyalty to his crewmen, his ship, and to the Federation. It is no wonder that Data is ostensibly a very popular character.

Another significant issue surrounding the viewing public's acceptance of Data as a person is that it reflects the popular and democratic idea that anyone is capable of meaningful speculation. The belief is that someone from any ethnicity or walk of life (even a machine) is able to *know* the absolute. Therefore, access to the *whole* is not limited to any ethnic group, "chosen people," or priesthood. More broadly, the Star Trek text (as outlined later) indicates that the purpose of humans is to speculate about the operation of the universe; societies; worlds—in other words, about everything. While love of knowledge (i.e., speculation) is posited as the highest form of human existence, romantic love is cast in a negative light—as a liability; a motive to break rules; and even as a form of slavery.[49]

Does human speculation in Star Trek, however, serve instrumental purposes, that is, empire building? I turn to this question next.

A FEDERATION EMPIRE?

Naeem Inayatullah in his essay "Bumpy Space: Imperialism and Resistance in *Star Trek: The Next Generation*"[50] seeks to link the Federation's mission to "seek out new life and new civilizations" with imperialism. In the episode "First Contact" (1991—*Next Generation*) the Chancellor of *Malcor 3*, upon first learning of the Federation and meeting Captain Picard, points out that "my world's history has recorded that conquerors often arrive with the words, 'We are your friends'." Captain Picard explains that "trust takes time and experience"—an ostensibly sensible response. Nevertheless, Inayatullah rather cynically holds that "Picard's answer obfuscates the critical issue: the hidden desires that lie beneath the apparently benevolent intentions of the Federation."[51] Why would Inayatuallah suggest that the Federation would have "hidden desires"? Inayatullah expressly conflates the Federation with Western imperialism: "In Western life, not much thought has gone into the desires and intentions of missionaries."[52] After expressly likening the American and British imperial projects to the Federation, Inayatullah writes "the dominance of the teaching drive over the need to learn sustains the usual props for benevolent imperialism."[53]

Inayatullah asks, "why engage"? the Malcorians and other societies on the verge of discovering warp speed—a velocity faster than light.[54] Inayatullah rejects the idea that helping a society into the fraternity of warp capable societies is necessary to harmonize relations between polities with such advanced capabilities—the reasoning offered by Picard. Instead, Inayatullah holds that Picard is murky in explaining why the Federation seeks to "guide" the Malcorians. Inayatullah appears intent on the idea that the only reason a power like that of the Federation would be interested in new peoples is imperialism—that is, resource exploitation and political hegemony. (Inayatuallah doesn't ask if the purpose of the Federation in "contacting" the Malcorians is motivated by imperial/hegemonic designs, why wait until the Malcorians are on the verge of warp speed capabilities?)

One point I make in *The Politics of Star Trek* is how shockingly (or willfully) ignorant of the Star Trek text its critics are. Arguably the most anti-imperialist episode ever on American television is the original series episode "Mirror, Mirror" (1967). "Mirror, Mirror" opens with a discussion between Captain Kirk and the leader of the "Halkans" (named "Tharn"). The Halkans refuse to allow the Federation to mine the dilithium crystals on their planet because "dilithium crystals represent awesome power. Wrongful use of that power, even to the extent of the taking of one life, would violate our history of total peace." Kirk asks "When may we resume discussion?" Tharn: "The council will meditate further, but do not be hopeful of any change." Tharn adds: "Captain, you do have the might to force the crystals from us, of course." Kirk: "But we won't."

Through a technical glitch, the Enterprise landing party is transported to an alternate universe. The Enterprise exists in this alternate universe, but instead of the Federation the political authority is the "Empire"— where "behavior and discipline" is "brutal, savage." While in the Federation universe the Enterprise only pursues peaceful means with the Halkans, in the Empire universe Kirk is "ordered to annihilate the Halkans unless they comply. *No alternative.*" Kirk (from the Federation universe) incurs great risks in an effort to prevent the destruction of the Halkans. "Mirror, Mirror" is an explicit rejection/critique of military intervention into other societies—particularly for purposes of controlling natural resources.

On the question of imperialism or hegemony with regard to the Federation, the original series episode "The Paradise Syndrome" (1968) is also noteworthy. The Enterprise crew comes upon a group of Native American tribes transported to an alien planet. ("A mixture of Navajo, Mohican, and Delaware, I believe. All among the more advanced and peaceful tribes.") Significantly, no effort whatsoever is made to colonize or interfere with the transported natives. Instead, Kirk *et al.* succeed in ensuring that the tribes can continue their premodern existence undisturbed.

STAR TREK AND THE "FEAR OF ERROR"

While Inayatullah's claim that the Federation is motived by empire building is baseless, his essay, nevertheless, invokes a good question: why do the humans in Star Trek venture into deep space? The creators point to speculation as the motivation underlying the Enterprise's deep space mission. The opening of the original series and *The Next Generation* famously attest to the fact that the franchise is predicated on speculative philosophy: the Enterprise's mission is "to boldly go whether no man/one has gone before." Hence, the crew of the Enterprise is exploring unknown regions of space where their knowledge about physical anomalies, cultures, etc. is minimal. In other words, they are going very far from home, where their knowledge of norms and metaphysics is more or less secure, and they are going into geographic regions where reliance on speculation has to regularly substitute for more seemingly reliable knowledge. Thus, in making the decision to explore space and "go where no one has gone before" is to consciously risk "error."

This brings us to the question of what does "fear of error" (rooted in analytic philosophy) in the realm of metaphysics really mean? That we don't know what we think we know? If so, then it is practically speaking trivial, as why does it really matter that we don't know what we think we know? We can still go on acting like we know, even if we actually don't. More substantially, the *fear of error* is the *fear of death*. Specifically, this means the fear that our flawed thinking about the world around us leads to our death and/or that of others. Hence, it appears the philosophical project focused solely on determining/exploring the reliability of knowledge (i.e., *categories*)—is primarily animated to avoid death.[55]

Star Trek indicates, however, that what humans value most is speculation and knowledge of the "absolute," and not life itself. Indeed, in Star Trek the characters by virtue of traveling in deep space, engaging the unknown, and relying on speculation, constantly risk death. In "Q Who?" (1989—*Next Generation*) the omnipotent "Q" introduces the Enterprise to the Borg (a technologically advanced, predatory species), which then results in the death of 18 crew members. Picard confronts Q about the death of these crew members. To which Q responds that exploring the galaxy is inherently dangerous: "If you can't take a little bloody nose, maybe you ought to go back home and crawl under your bed. It's not safe out here." Picard seemingly agrees by remaining silent. Additionally, Picard later holds that "Maybe Q did the right thing" in exposing the Enterprise to the Borg as meeting the Borg alerted the Federation to their prowess: "what we most needed was a kick in our complacency, to prepare us ready for what lies ahead." Put differently, prompting humanity to speculate about the Borg overshadows the loss of life following the Enterprise's encounter with them.

The ostensive importance of being willing to sacrifice oneself for a greater purpose (e.g., gaining knowledge) is succinctly and artfully conveyed in the 1982 movie *Star Trek: Wrath of Kahn* when David tells his grieving father, Captain Kirk (over Spock's death), that "how we face death is at least as important as how we face life." In other words, to live a meaningful (even enjoyable) life people have to be ready to die for just/ appropriate causes.

The franchise makes the sustained argument that existentially humans prioritize the attainment of justice (fairness) over concerns of death. For instance, in the original series episode "Cloud Minders" (1969) Captain Kirk decides to try to improve the lives of the mine working "Troglytes" on "Ardana" even though he is explicitly warned that by seeking to do so he risks execution.

One (perhaps generous) view of humanity is that people prefer death rather than endure pronounced/obvious injustice. This view is vaunted in the Star Trek original unaired pilot "The Cage."[56] A powerful alien race is planning on breeding and exploiting humans. They, however, come to conclude that humans are not appropriate for such a project because they cannot be adapted to unjust circumstances (specifically, imposed captivity): "We had not believed this possible. The customs and history of your race show a unique hatred of captivity. Even when it's pleasant and benevolent, you prefer death. This makes you too violent and dangerous a species for our needs."

Indeed, Star Trek goes further and explicitly takes the position that death is a normative good. The fact that humans know that their life is finite prompts them to seek to forward knowledge and justice (what is described below as the *progressive dialectic*). Put differently, death makes life valuable, and realizing how little life people have makes them to want to use this time as productively as possible—i.e., actively participating in the progressive dialectic. This argument is outlined in "Tapestry" (1993—*Next Generation*). Captain Picard as a young cadet in Starfleet Academy engaged in a fight that resulted in his being stabbed in the heart, which was then replaced with a mechanical one. Some thirty years later, as Captain of the Enterprise Picard subsequently dies because of his artificial heart. Q intervenes and allows Picard to relive the events that led to his stabbing. Picard takes this opportunity and never gets stabbed, nor receives a mechanical heart—allowing him to putatively keep living beyond the accident that later kills him. After Picard avoids getting stabbed, Q returns him to the present where he finds he is no longer Captain of the Enterprise and determines that he does not like himself now: "I can't live out my days as that person. That man is bereft of passion and imagination. That is not who I am." Q explains to Picard that without coming close to death (with his "Nausicaan" impaling) he remained rather inured to the reality that the opportunities to contribute to the progressive dialectic are inherently finite:

> The Jean-Luc Picard you wanted to be, the one who did not fight the Nausicaan, had quite a different career from the one you remember. That Picard never had a brush with death, never came face to face with his own mortality, never realized how fragile life is or how important each moment must be. So his life never came into focus. He drifted for much of his career, with no plan or agenda, going from one assignment to the next, never seizing the opportunities that presented themselves...And no one ever offered him a command. He learned to play it safe. And he never, ever got noticed by anyone.

In the end, Picard chooses death over living life as what he perceives as a minimal contributor to the progressive dialectic: "I would rather die as the man I was than live the life I just saw."

Birth, as death, is a normative good. Birth allows individuals to experience the progressive dialectic anew. Birth also brings new people, ideas into the dialectical process. When the Q Continuum suffers a civil war the resolution is to give birth to new Q that will re-energize an otherwise stagnating Continuum: "I don't see how a baby is going to end a war...?" "What the Continuum needs right now is an infusion of fresh blood, a new sensibility..." ("The Q and the Grey" 1996—*Voyager*).

Birth and death are also normative goods because they are central to the operation of the dialectic. This is because the progressive dialectic operates through evolution—a continual cycle of life and death. Star Trek points to the "pond of goo" from which all life on Earth, including humanity, evolved ("All Good Things..." 1994—*Next Generation*; see Figure 1 in the Preface).

Star Trek tells us that humanity is evolving toward a higher state of being (see Chapter 2). Thus, going "to explore strange new worlds; to seek out new life and new civilizations" and by consciously risking death (i.e., relying heavily on speculation) humanity will attain presumably a higher consciousness—i.e., complete knowledge of the *absolute*, or the *whole*. Therefore, speculation is humanity's natural state, and a focus on the reliability of categories (i.e., analytic philosophy) is misplaced—as human evolution points directly toward speculative reasoning and a fixation on categories is predicated on fear of death, when in fact humans don't really fear death but the lack of new knowledge and justice.

While Star Trek is centered on love of knowledge and justice, selfishness is cast negatively—including romantic love. Expressing the selfless politics of the twenty-third century, Captain Kirk: "*Let me help*. A hundred years or so from now...a famous novelist will write a classic using that theme. He'll recommend those three words even over *I love you*."[57] Romantic love is depicted as secondary to the quest for the absolute, unnecessary for a fulfilling life, something of a liability, and as enslavement itself. The relative unimportance of romantic love in Star Trek is indicated by the fact that very few of the characters in the Star Trek franchise are married, or in a long term relationship. Only one captain of the five Star Trek television series was married (Sisko—*Deep Space Nine*), and in the denouement of the show he leaves his wife (who was pregnant at the time) indefinitely to gain knowledge of non-corporal entities (the Bajoran "Prophets") ("What You Leave Behind" 1999—*Deep Space Nine*).

STAR TREK AND ROMANTIC LOVE

In addition to being about the quest for knowledge, Star Trek is about non-biological relationships—not informed by biology nor marriage. At the center of the Star Trek franchise is the claim that non-biological family relations are just as valid and fulfilling as relations informed by biology or marriage. The relationship between Kirk, Spock, and McCoy is as vital and emotionally intimate as any relationship conveyed on American television (perhaps more so). A similar argument can be made of all Star Trek series—where few characters are married or have children and same sex friendships are the norm.

While Kirk is an infamous philanderer, David Greven, in his outstanding book *Gender and Sexuality in Star Trek*, makes the effective argument that Kirk's trysts were mostly cast as exotic and extraneous—and generally do not achieve the depth of feeling that Kirk, Spock, and McCoy have. The one exception to this is Kirk's relationship with Edith Keeler (played wonderfully by Joan Collins) in "City on the Edge of Forever" (1967—original series). With Kirk and Spock down and out in New York City during the Great Depression of the 1930s, Keeler's kindness, charity, and idealism render her very endearing and attractive to the audience as a well as to Kirk. Kirk and Keeler share the same social justice values:

Edith:	I think that one day they'll take all the money they spend now on war and death
Kirk:	And make them spend it on life?
Edith:	Yes. You see the same things that I do. We speak the same language.
Kirk:	The very same.

It appears as quite natural when Kirk declares his love for Keeler.

Alas, it was not meant to be, as Keeler's fate is emblematic of the Star Trek motif of romantic love as a liability. Kirk and Spock came to 1930s New York to restore the Federation, as McCoy's intervention into the past somehow upended Earth's history—"Your vessel, your beginning, all that you knew is gone." Kirk and Spock follow McCoy into the past to undo the damage he's done. As it turns out, Edith Keeler is a "focal point in time." McCoy prevents her from dying in an accident and she subsequently sparks a pacifist movement that blocks the U.S. entrance into World War II—thereby allowing the Nazis to win the war. Kirk and Spock determine that "Edith Keeler must die," and they need to prevent McCoy from saving her life. Kirk's romantic feelings for her, however, jeopardize their mission. Spock expresses concern that Kirk is not emotionally capable of allowing Keeler to die. To Kirk: "Save her, do as your heart tells you to do, and millions will die who did not die before."

An instance of romantic love resulting in the breaking of rules is the *Star Trek: Deep Space Nine* (1993–1999) episode "Change of Heart" (1998). Worf and Dax, who are married, are sent on a mission that could end the *Dominion War*. Dax however becomes injured and Worf decides to abandon the mission (and disregard his orders) to save her, thereby losing the opportunity to deliver a decisive blow to the *Dominion*—he "could have saved millions of lives." It was Worf's romantic love for Dax that resulted in his fateful decision: "I could not stand against my own heart. *It did not matter...what the consequences were*. She was my wife and I could not leave her."

Q in "Qpid" (1991—*Next Generation*) expressly describes romantic love as a "vulnerability": "This human emotion, love, is a dangerous thing, Picard, and obviously you are ill-equipped to handle it. She's found a vulnerability in you. A vulnerability I've been looking for for years...Mark my words, Picard, this is your Achilles heel." Q later adds: (to Picard) "My point is they could have been killed, and so might have you. All for the love of a maid."

Romantic love in "Elaan of Troyius" (1968—original series) is explicitly described as a form of slavery: "A man whose flesh is once touched by the tears of a woman of Elas has his heart enslaved forever." Kirk wipes away the tears of "Elaan" and comes under her spell as a result. But in the end, Kirk's love of knowledge and justice overcomes his chemically induced "love" for Elaan: Spock: "The antidote to a woman of Elas...is a starship. The Enterprise infected the Captain long before [she] did."

CONCLUSION

While speculation is deemed central to humanity's evolutionary process and humans' *authenticity*[58], Star Trek makes the argument that the *absolute* operates as a *progressive dialectic*. Therefore, when we speculate and garner knowledge we are fulfilling the promise of the *absolute*, which is rational and leading humanity toward a classless society, free of gender/ethnic biases. We speculate and achieve this knowledge in spite of the risk of death—sometimes in spite of romantic love. Therefore, analytic philosophy, and its fear of error, is misplaced because humans' existentially fear lack of knowledge of the absolute more than they fear error and the death that can result from error.

As indicated earlier, Star Trek is not limited to arguments about personal knowledge, enlightenment, and fulfillment. The franchise makes the broader claim humanity can only thrive (and perhaps survive) if it collectively pursues the *progressive dialectic*—presumably the absolute *writ large*.

CHAPTER 4

The Progressive Dialectic of Star Trek

Abstract The progressive dialectic was initially identified by Karl Marx and later acted upon by Leon Trotsky. The progressive dialectic is artistically represented in the *United Federation of Planets*—the fictional interstellar political entity in Star Trek that humans lead. The failure to speculate about the absolute and pursue the progressive dialectic is to precipitate disaster for humanity. Star Trek, in artistically conveying the progressive dialectic, makes the specific argument that if humanity/civilization is to survive/thrive, then capitalist values have to be abandoned and neoliberalism has to be replaced.

Keywords Georg Hegel · The Absolute · Star Trek · Karl Marx · Leon Trotsky

The *progressive dialectic* was initially identified by Karl Marx and later acted upon by Leon Trotsky. The progressive dialectic is artistically represented in the *United Federation of Planets*—the fictional interstellar political entity in Star Trek that humans lead. The failure to speculate about the *absolute* and pursue the *progressive dialectic* is to precipitate disaster for humanity. Star Trek, in artistically conveying the progressive dialectic, makes the specific argument that if humanity/civilization is to survive/thrive then capitalist values have to be abandoned and neoliberalism has to be replaced.

© The Author(s) 2017
G.A. Gonzalez, *The Absolute and Star Trek*,
DOI 10.1007/978-3-319-47794-7_4

STAR TREK AND CAPITALISM

Star Trek explicitly rejects capitalism in *The Next Generation* episode "The Neutral Zone" (1988). A wealthy business owner, named "Ralph Offenhouse," from the late-twentieth century is revived from a cryogenic chamber floating in space. (*The Next Generation* takes place in the twenty-fourth century.) Upon being awoken, Ralph explains that "I have a substantial portfolio. It's critical I check on it." Later, he adds, "I have to phone Geneva right away about my accounts. The interest alone could be enough to buy even this ship." Ralph dons an attitude of arrogance, entitlement, and authority. He tells Captain Picard, "I demand you see me." When Picard tries to put Ralph off by referring to the sensitive situation the ship is dealing with at the time, Ralph retorts, "I'm sure that whatever it is seems very important to you. My situation is far more critical." Ralph condescends the Captain: "It is simply that I have more to protect than a man in your position could possibly imagine. No offense, but a military career has never been considered upwardly mobile." Picard, losing his patience, informs Ralph that his value system (and attitude) is misplaced and disdained in the current epoch:

> *Picard*:   A lot has changed in three hundred years. People are no longer obsessed with the accumulation of "things." We have eliminated hunger, want, the need for possessions. We have grown out of our infancy.
>
> *Ralph*:   You've got it wrong. It's never been about "possessions"—it's about power.[59]
>
> *Picard*:   Power to do what?
>
> *Ralph*:   To control your life, your destiny.
>
> *Picard*:   That kind of control is an illusion.

Chastened, Ralph asks, "There's no trace of my money—my office is gone—what will I do? How will I live?" Picard explains "Those material needs no longer exist." Ralph, invoking the values of the late twentieth century, responds by asking: "Then what's the challenge?" Picard, seemingly outlining the values of twenty-fourth-century Earth, retorts: "To improve yourself . . . enrich yourself. Enjoy it, Mister Offenhouse."

Similarly, in the *Deep Space Nine* episode "In the Cards" (1997), Jake Sisko exclaims, "I'm Human, I don't have any money." Nog, a Ferengi—an alien race that operates on the profit-motive—is critical of twenty-fourth-century humanity: "It's not my fault that your species decided to abandon currency-based economics in favor of some philosophy of self-enhancement." Shifting humanity's (America's) values away from "currency-based economics" and toward a "philosophy of self-enhancement" mirrors Karl Marx's point that in moving from capitalism to communism, society would go "From each according to his ability, to each according to his needs!"—that is, communist politics would focus on "the all-around development of the individual."[60] Or as Jake told Nog: "There's nothing wrong with our philosophy. We work to better ourselves and the rest of Humanity."

Indicative of how humans in the twenty-fourth century have undergone a profound paradigm shift in values and outlook, Quark, a Ferengi who traveled back to mid-twentieth-century Earth (more specifically, the United States), concludes from his dealings with humans (Americans) in this epoch, that "these humans, they're not like the ones from the [twenty-fourth-century] Federation. They're crude, gullible and greedy" ("Little Green Men" 1995—*Deep Space Nine*). Marx offers a consonant rebuke of the cultural/social ethos of capitalists: "Contempt for theory, art, history, and for man as an end in himself... is the real, conscious standpoint, the virtue of the man of money."[61]

Therefore, Star Trek takes the Enlightenment to its logical conclusion—namely, that modernity; science; reason can serve as the basis for a peaceful; highly productive; and thriving world. Star Trek is optimistic insofar as arguing that as global society accepts modernity; reason; science (i.e., the progressive dialectic) humans will collectively achieve a higher plane of intelligence; knowledge; and emotional immaturity. (An optimism shared by Marx: in "communist society... the all-round development of the individual" will be achieved.[62]) This higher plane of existence, however, requires the overthrow of the neoliberal order.

Neoliberalism

To the American Revolutionary War (see later in the text), the U.S. Civil War (see later in the text), and the American fight against Fascism ("City on the Edge of Forever" 1967—original series), Star Trek adds to America's revolutionary "moments" with the *Bell Uprising*. Aired in 1995, "Past Tense" (*Deep Space Nine*) is centered on this fictional uprising. The characters Sisko, Bashir, and Dax are accidentally sent back to 2024 San Francisco, where, like in "City on the Edge of Forever," they alter Earth's history for the worse. Upon being beamed to the past, Sisko and Bashir are separated from Dax. Without any identification (or money) Sisko and Bashir are forcibly interned in an urban detainment camp for the poor and dispossessed—a *Sanctuary District*. It is described in script notes as follows:

> Sisko and Bashir ENTER a street lined by dirty, dilapidated buildings, with boarded up windows and impromptu campsites set up in the doorways and stairwells. It's a sharp contrast to the relatively clean city outside. The street is crowded with poorly dressed homeless men, women, and children, of all ages and races, many standing in a long food line.[63]

Sisko, who is knowledgeable about twenty-first-century Earth, explains that "by the early twenty-twenties there was a place like this in every major city in the United States."

Bashir asks:	Why are these people in here? Are they criminals?
Sisko:	No. People with criminal records weren't allowed in the Sanctuary Districts.
Bashir:	Then what did they do to deserve this?
Sisko:	Nothing. They're just people. People without jobs or places to live.
Bashir:	So they get put in here?
Sisko:	Welcome to the twenty-first century.

Writing in the mid-1990s about internment camps for the poor and homeless being in place in every major American city within 30 years is an explicit critique of the neoliberal project, which was well established by the 1990s.[64] Neoliberalism, whose proponents prioritize the free movement of capital, goods, and services, has been devastating to numerous U.S. urban centers, particularly in the former industrial American heartland.[65] Cities like Detroit[66] and Cleveland[67]—which were global centers of industrial production—have been hollowed out as the U.S. manufacturing base has been shifted to cheap wage venues in the U.S. South; Mexico; China, etc.[68] One of the displaced residents of the San Francisco Sanctuary District explains that "I used to be a Plant Manager at ChemTech Industries." The result has been pronounced urban decay in once wealthy and prosperous cities,[69] where a substantial homeless population is an enduring phenomenon.[70]

Moreover, the Great Recession of 2008 has caused persistently high unemployment.[71] A historically de-stabilizing factor of capitalism is the tendency of capital equipment (i.e., technology) to replace labor.[72] In a 2012 op-ed piece in the *New York Times*, the Princeton economist Paul

Krugman holds "there's no question that in some high-profile industries, technology is displacing workers of all, or almost all, kinds."[73] A Sanctuary District resident explains that "I came to San Francisco to work in a brewery . . . but they laid a bunch of us off when they got some new equipment . . . and so I ended up here." Another of the characters in "Past Tense" notes that "right now jobs are hard to come by . . . what with the economy and all . . ." The former plant manager plaintively explains: "Most of us agreed to live here [in the San Francisco Sanctuary District] because they promised us jobs. I don't know about you, but I haven't been on any job interviews lately. And neither has anyone else. They've forgotten about us."

TROTSKYISM AND THE PROGRESSIVE DIALECTIC

The overriding need to pursue societal justice (i.e., topple neoliberalism/ capitalism) is made clear in "Past Tense." While in the Sanctuary District (in 2024 San Francisco) Sisko intervenes into a fight, which accidently results in the death of one Gabriel Bell—the would-be leader of the Bell Uprising. Like the victory of the Nazis in World War II ("City on the Edge of Forever"), this erases the entire history of the Federation. Meanwhile, back in the twenty-fourth century, all that remains of the original time line is the ship (the Defiant) that beamed Sisko, Bashir, and Dax to the past. Uncertain when Sisko *et al.* are located, members of the Defiant crew randomly transport into Earth's past. They conclude Sisko *et al.* "arrived before the year twenty-forty-eight."

> How can you be sure?
>   Because we were just there. And that wasn't the mid-twenty-first century that I read about in school. It's been changed. *Earth history had its rough patches, but never that rough.*

Therefore, the absence of the Bell Uprising to spark the revolution that would politically challenge the current neoliberalism regime would ostensibly result in Earth's society devolving into some type of nightmare scenario as early as 2048. One is reminded of Rosa Luxemburg's pronouncement that the "future is either socialism or barbarism."[74]

The original time line is restored when Sisko takes the name Gabriel Bell, and fulfills his role in history. One of the successes of the Bell Uprising was the ability of residents of the Sanctuary District to evade a government blockade of the "Interface" (i.e., the internet—which was a nascent technology when "Past Tense" aired in 1995) and convey their personal stories to the world. One resident explains: "My name is Henry Garcia and I've been living here two years now . . . I've never been in trouble with the law or anything . . . I don't want to hurt anybody . . . I just want a chance to work and live like regular people."

Confirming the interpretation of Star Trek as positing American history as a series of progressive events ("revolutions") is "The Savage Curtain" (1969—original series) and "The Omega Glory" (1968—original series). The episode "The Omega Glory" depicts a world with an identical history to that of Earth's, except in this instance the Cold War resulted in globally devastating nuclear/biological war—where humans were reduced to a veritable stone age. Kirk ultimately realizes that the segment of the population that represented the West views the U.S. Constitution as a sacred document. But they cannot read it, so Kirk explains to them: "That which you called Ee'd Plebnista was not written for chiefs or kings or warriors or the rich and powerful, but for all the people!" Kirk proceeds to read directly from this document (the Ee'd Plebnista), which is the Constitution:

> We the people of the United States, in order to form a more perfect union, establish justice, ensure domestic tranquility, provide for the common defense, promote the general welfare, and secure the blessings of liberty to ourselves and our posterity . . . do ordain and establish this constitution.

Asserting the revolutionary implications of the American Revolution and the Constitution that followed, Kirk declares, "these words and the words that follow . . . They must apply to everyone or they mean nothing!" Kirk adds, "liberty and freedom have to be more than just words."

In "The Savage Curtain" the Enterprise crew meets the incarnation of Abraham Lincoln. While acknowledging that this is not the real Lincoln, Kirk insists that the crew treat him with the respect and deference due this great historical figure—the leader of what many consider to be the second American Revolution (i.e., the victorious Northern Cause in the U.S. Civil War).[75] Kirk notes: "I cannot conceive it possible that Abraham Lincoln . . . could have actually been reincarnated. And yet his kindness, his gentle wisdom, his humor, everything about him is so right." McCoy chides Kirk: "Practically the entire crew has seen you treat this impostor like the real thing . . . when he can't possibly be the real article. [. . .] Lincoln died three centuries ago hundreds of light-years away." Spock observes to Kirk: "President Lincoln has always been a very personal hero to you." Kirk retorts: "Not only to me." Spock: "Agreed."

Thus, Star Trek is optimistic in that America is evolving toward an ideal, classless society. The American Revolution; the Civil War; the Fight Against Fascism; the Bell Uprising (i.e., the defeat of neoliberalism) are necessary stops on this road to (worldwide) utopia. This is reflective of American Marxists' view that U.S. history is an unfolding revolutionary process, the end result of which is the establishment of an ideal socialist/communist society. Sidney Hook, for instance, writing in 1933 (when he was still a Troskyist) reasoned that "America had gone through her second revolution to break up the semi-feudal slavocracy which barred the expansion of industrial capitalism."[76] Operating in the United States since the 1920s, Trotskyists hold that the American Revolution and the Civil War remain incomplete until the worker state is in place.[77] Put differently, these revolutions will be completed by the socialist revolution (the Bell Uprising[?]). (It is noteworthy and significant that in the episode where the Bell Uprising is conveyed, the phrase "Neo-Trotskists" is used; also, in another episode, a passage from the Communist Manifesto is read.[78])

CONCLUSION

According to Star Trek, Karl Marx was right. The absolute is pointing toward the rejection of capitalist values. Moreover, modern neoliberalism must be replaced if humanity is to thrive. Therefore, the absolute is rational and leading humanity toward a classless society, free of gender and ethnic biases.

Like Hegel does, Star Trek warns against false infinities, which would lead humanity away from the absolute and toward disaster. As shown above, neoliberalism is a *false infinity*. Next, I point to specific philosophers, which according to Star Trek also counsel what are false infinities.

CHAPTER 5

Star Trek and False Infinities

Abstract Star Trek, through fictional narrative, conveys what is the prime philosophical debate of the modern era. On the one hand, there is Karl Marx and his prominent revolutionary acolyte, Leon Trotsky (with Star Trek's creators making direct reference to both Marx and Trotsky—as noted in Chapter 4). On the other hand, there is Friedrich Nietzsche, Martin Heidegger, Carl Schmitt, and Leo Strauss. To invoke Star Wars, these latter thinkers represent the "Dark Side" of the "Force." Or in Hegelian terms, they represent *false infinities*. Put differently, Star Trek warns that to pursue the philosophical ideation set out by Nietzsche *et al.* is to engage racism, xenophobia, and ultimately the end of human civilization.

Keywords Georg Hegel · Friedrich Nietzsche · Martin Heidegger · Carl Schmitt · Leo Strauss · Star Trek

Star Trek, through fictional narrative, conveys what is the prime philosophical debate of the modern era. On the one hand, there is Karl Marx and his prominent revolutionary acolyte, Leon Trotsky (with Star Trek's creators making direct reference to both Marx and Trotsky—as noted in Chapter 4). On the other hand, there is Friedrich Nietzsche, Martin Heidegger, Carl Schmitt, and Leo Strauss. To invoke Star Wars, these latter thinkers represent the "Dark Side" of the "Force." Or in

© The Author(s) 2017
G.A. Gonzalez, *The Absolute and Star Trek*,
DOI 10.1007/978-3-319-47794-7_5

Hegelian-like terms, they represent *false infinities*.[79] Put differently, Star Trek warns that to pursue the philosophical ideation set out by Nietzsche *et al.* is to engage racism, xenophobia, and ultimately the end of human civilization.

It is particularly significant that according to Star Trek a victory by the Nazis during World War II would have meant the end of civilization ("City on the Edge of Forever" 1967—original series; see Chapter 3). The positive relationship of Heidegger[80] and Schmitt[81] to the Nazis regime is well documented. Additionally, while Strauss was Jewish and exiled from Nazi Germany, he was nevertheless attracted to and inspired by the ideation of Heidegger and Schmitt.[82] Moreover, it is significant that Nietzsche was viewed favorably by the Hitler regime.[83] What these thinkers and the Nazis have in common is, to varying degrees, an overt hostility to the progressive dialectic philosophized upon by Marx; acted upon by Trotsky; and fictionally/aesthetically portrayed in Star Trek (see Chapter 4). The Nazi project, I would argue, was specifically geared toward negating the progressive dialectic (the "Triumph of the Will"[84]), or more specifically, drowning the progressive dialectic in blood and suppressing it through a sustained regime of terror and violence. The Nazis' hateful attitude toward the progressive dialectic was manifest in its venom (to put it mildly) toward Marxism, Bolshevism, and, Jews, more broadly[85]— who were viewed as the intellectual bearers of the progressive dialectic.

Again, Star Trek makes the specific, precise claim that a Nazi military/political victory would mean the end of civilization. Thus, Star Trek makes the overt argument that the choice between Marx *et al.* and Nietzsche *et al.* is not simply a matter of subjective normative predilections, but a choice between the survival and thriving of humanity and human civilization or their imminent destruction.

Nietzsche, of course, denies the idea that a progressive dialectic empirically/metaphysically exists—instead, reality (and human society) is a perpetual cycle of destruction and rejuvenation.[86] Star Trek, again, makes the claim that the progressive dialectic does exist. Through such episodes as "City on the Edge of Forever" and "Past Tense" (1995—*Deep Space Nine*) Star Trek shows us that the failure to bring the dialectic to fruition means the end of civilization.

Next, contrary to reasoning posited by Heidegger, Star Trek demonstrates that death is a normative good—a valuable end of consciousness, and plays a central and critical role in the progressive dialectic. I follow this by outlining how Star Trek shows that Schmitt's notion of the *other* invokes political instability (political racism), and, in the modern era, directly creates the risk of planetary destruction. Leo Strauss held that society should return to premodern ideas of political religion (theocracy). Star Trek expressly rejects such a proposal, as theocracy is inherently dangerous and stunts the human intellect.

DEATH, BIRTH, AND THE PROGRESSIVE DIALECTIC

Heidegger makes the rather cynical claim that concepts of justice, fairness, and equality are little more than efforts by people to evade the fact that their life is finite (death). Universal ideas (justice, etc.) only create the illusion that our lives have meaning beyond the grave.[87] Star Trek, however, shows us that people are willing to die to protect/forward the progressive dialectic. Star Trek points to the American Revolutionary War (see earlier in the text), the U.S. Civil War (see earlier in the text), and the Fight Against Fascism ("City on the Edge of Forever"), where soldiers died in the tens-of-thousands, hundreds-of-thousands, and millions to forward/protect the progressive dialectic. Judging from these wars, it does not appear that people are so scared of death, as they are of the failure of the progressive dialectic.

Star Trek is explicitly critical of those that would prioritize life (i.e., pacifism) over the progressive dialectic. In "City on the Edge of Forever" it is the pacifism of Edith Keeler that blocks the entrance of the United States into World War II and allows the Nazis to win. An obvious rebuke of pacifism to maintain life (i.e., avoiding war) is offered in the 1990 *Next Generation* episode "Allegiance" (1990). Captain Picard, along with someone from the planet "Mizar Two," is being held captive. The character from Mizar Two (a "Mizarian")—with some pride—alludes to his planet's pacifist tradition: "My race has no enemies." Picard, incredulously, retorts: "*None?*... In the last three hundred years of Mizarian history, your planet has been conquered six times!" Arguing that pacifism preserves life, the Mizarian (named "Tholl") explains that "we've survived by not resisting." Finally, Tholl holds that pacifism is morally superior to fighting for democracy, freedom, equality, etc.: "Mizarians value peace above confrontation." One of the other captives denounces Mizarians as "A race of cowards"— the viewer cannot help but to agree.

Moreover, in a direct rebuke of Heidegger's reasoning, Star Trek demonstrates that people do not fear death, but eternal life. The *Voyager* episode "Death Wish" (1996) centers on a member of the *Q Continuum* that wants to die. The Q are immortal. After living for time immemorial, and experiencing virtually everything, a member of the Q, "Quinn," is longing for death. ("The one thing I want more than any other, is to die.") Quinn wants to die because immortally has resulted in mind numbing, inescapable boredom: "Because it has all been said. Everyone has heard everything, seen everything. They [the members of the Q Continuum] haven't had to speak to each other in ten millennia. There's nothing left to say."

Thus, contrary to Heidegger's thinking, individuals do not measure success in life by their longevity, but by how they contribute to the progressive dialectic. Star Trek indicates that the basis of the progressive dialectic is honesty, selflessness, and intellectual, scientific discovery/knowledge. These are the values at the core of the Federation.

With the 1996 movie *First Contact*, Star Trek explores another basis of political legitimation (apart from the progressive dialectic)—the concept of the "other." Hence, following this movie, the series *Enterprise* is predicated on Carl Schmitt's notions of political stability and legitimacy. While *Enterprise* artistically conveys a political regime based on the *other*, it also actively warns against such politics. Specifically, the claim is made that using the concept of the "other" (in this case Vulcans) as the basis of a polity results in divisiveness and even racism (as evident in the *Enterprise* episode "Terra Prime" 2005). Moreover, a planet permanently cleaved into competing polities (or "others") portends planetary destruction (i.e., the Xindi).

THE "FRIEND/ENEMY" DICHOTOMY AND STAR TREK

Carl Schmitt (1888–1985) was an architect of the Nazi Germany legal regime and known as the "Crown Jurist" of the Nazis.[88] Schmitt held that at the center of politics is the distinction "between friend and enemy."[89] Political theorist Shadia B. Drury renders the following observation: "Schmitt . . . believe[d] that politics is first and foremost about the distinction between WE and THEY. [He] thinks that a political order can be stable only if it is united by an external threat."[90] Reflective of Schmitt's "friend/enemy" reasoning, in *The Next Generation* episode "Face of the Enemy" (1993) the point is made that Romulans have an "absolute certainty about . . . who is a friend and who is an enemy." The main component of Hitler's and the Nazis' political/propaganda argumentation was directed at an imaginary coalition of Western bankers and Eastern communists conspiring against Germany. According to Nazi mythology (myopia) Jews were at the center of this worldwide anti-Germany coalition. In the face of this global conspiracy directed against Germany, the Hitler regime argued that the German people must be unified (i.e., no dissent whatsoever), and strike back (i.e., World War II).[91]

The Star Trek movie *First Contact* (1996) is predicated on a WE/THEY distinction. The action of the movie takes place in the year 2063. The Borg go back in Earth's history to prevent humanity's first contact with the Vulcans. This initial exposure to an alien culture occurs because Zephran Cochrane conducts humanity's first successful warp drive experiment. (*Warp speed* represents a speed faster than light.) When the Vulcans detect Cochrance's ship achieving warp speed they decide to introduce themselves to earthlings—"first contact." In this iteration (*First Contact*) of Star Trek's historiography of Earth in 2063 humanity is in what is referred to a "Second Dark Age."[92] What rallies humanity from its disarray is its contact with the Vulcans: "*It unites humanity in a way no one ever thought possible when they realize they're not alone in the universe.*"

Therefore, the political foundation of humanity in the mid-twenty-first century is the WE/THEY dichotomy—with the Vulcans serving as *They.* "The political enemy is not necessarily morally evil." Instead, Schmitt held that the potential enemy "is merely the other, the stranger, and it is sufficient that according to his nature he is in a special intense way existentially something different and alien, so that in the extreme case conflicts with him are possible."[93]

In *Enterprise* conflict with the Vulcans does occur. "The Andorian Incident" (2001) concludes with the exposure of a Vulcan "spy station" by Captain Archer, which earns the ire of the Vulcans. The Vulcan ambassador to Earth complains that "the Andorians wouldn't have found the [spy] station if your people hadn't interfered." The Enterprise has "been in space for six months and they've already destabilized an entire sector" ("Shadows of P'Jem" 2002). "Fusion" (2002) involves a set of Vulcans, who contrary to Vulcan norms, embrace their emotions. ("I always knew there had to be more to life than just logic and reason.") One of these Vulcans telepathically "rapes" T'Pol (a Vulcan and Enterprise's first officer), and Captain Archer engages in an intense fist fight with the transgressor. "The Forge"(2004), "Awakening"(2004), and the "Kir'Shara"(2004) is a three episode story arc whereby Earth's embassy on Vulcan is bombed, killing Admiral Forrest (Archer's mentor), and the Enterprise crew gets swept up in internal Vulcan religious and political strife—with an effort made against Captain Archer's life; and the Enterprise and Vulcan military ships coming to a face-off. In the denouement we learn that elements within the Vulcan government were behind the bombing of the Earth embassy, and that a faction still in the government wants to pull the planet toward a political/military alliance with the Romulans—an intention ominously threatening to Earth.

The WE/THEY or friend/foe dichotomy at the heart of Earth's politics in *Enterprise*, and *First Contact*, is in sharp contrast to earlier iterations of Star Trek, where state-building was accomplished through the progressive expansion of political rights and social justice: the American Revolution ("The Omega Glory" 1968—original series); the U.S. Civil War ("The Savage Curtain" 1969—original series); the Fight Against Fascism ("City on the Edge of Forever"); and the "Bell Uprising" ("Past Tense"). Such an ontology of social/political change (i.e., through revolutionary moments/events)—as noted above—is entirely consistent (if not inspired) by classic Marxism.[94]

It is significant that in *First Contact* by 2063 San Francisco is destroyed.[95] In "Past Tense" San Francisco is where the anti-neoliberalist *Bell Uprising* occurs in 2024 (i.e., the basis of a new global politics).

"Terra Prime" and the Xindi

The *Enterprise* series concludes in 2005 and the penultimate episode "Terra Prime" centers on the group Terra Prime. Initially, this organization is described as xenophobic: "They want to stop all contact with alien species." "They believe it's corrupting our way of life." Terra Prime "had a resurgence following the Xindi attack" on Earth. Later, we learn that Terra Prime is racist: "This is an alien-human hybrid. Living proof of what will happen if we allow ourselves to be submerged in an interstellar coalition. Our genetic heritage..." "That child is a cross-breed freak. How many generations before our genome is so diluted that the word human is nothing more than a footnote in some medical text?" The leader of Terra Prime declares "I'm returning Earth to its rightful owners."

The group seeks to scuttle the formation of the Federation by promising to destroy Starfleet command (in San Francisco) unless all aliens leave Earth. Referring to signs of popular support for Terra Prime and its agenda, the Vulcan Ambassador Soval notes: "The fact that Paxton has the support of so many of your people is...troubling."

An Andorian ambassador makes the point that: "Earthmen talk about uniting worlds, but your own planet is deeply divided. Perhaps you're not quite ready to host this conference" promoting interstellar cooperation.

Of great significance for a discussion based on Schmitt's vision of politics informed by the idea of the *other*, is the Xindi—introduced in *Enterprise*. The Xindi are the former inhabitants of the planet Xindi. The Xindi are cleaved into five distinct polities, with each polity corresponding to a distinct species: one insectoid; one humanoid; aquatic; ape-like; and reptilian. As a result of their division/competition, the Xindi destroyed their own planet: "The war went on for nearly a hundred years.... The insectoids and reptilians detonated massive explosions beneath the eight largest seismic fissures. I'd like to think they didn't realize how devastating the result would be."[96]

Leo Strauss and "The Apple"

Leo Strauss, like Nietzsche, Heidegger, and Schmitt, rejected the progressive dialectic. In Strauss's case, he held that society should revert to premodern times. Specifically, Strauss argued for a polity based explicitly on religion, and the philosopher should have an autonomous role in society—thereby serving as a perennial critic (gadfly), in order to (ideally) prevent corruption and excessive repression.[97]

Star Trek casts political religion as dangerous and stunting human intellectual development.[98] Hence, political religion (theocracy) is something to be avoided. "All Our Yesterdays" (1969—original series) is an episode where Captain Kirk is transported back to the Puritan period, and comes close to being burned alive for being a "witch." When the Enterprise is involved in rekindling religious beliefs among a group of primitive people, the point is made "that religion could degenerate into inquisitions, holy wars, chaos" ("Who Watches the Watchers" 1989— *Next Generation*).

Perhaps the strongest critique of theocracy in the history of American television is posited in "The Apple" (1967—original series). The primitive people of a planet worship a machine, *Vaal*. The "people of Vaal" provide it with energy (food) and Vaal provides for all their needs and protects them from disease and even death. Significantly, the people of Vaal are quite dimwitted, as they are completely dependent on Vaal and unable to take care of themselves. Kirk makes the following observation of the natives: "These people aren't living, they're existing. They don't create, they don't produce, they don't even think. They exist to service a machine." Thus, it is preferable to struggle for survival and develop your mind and society as a result, than it is to live in comfort but in ignorance. Hence, despite Spock's claim that the Enterprise crew drove the people of Vaal out of "Eden," Doctor McCoy confidently holds "we put those people back on a normal course of social evolution"—that is, the progressive dialectic.

CONCLUSION

Star Trek is a sacred text—informing humanity of the progressive dialectic. This dialectic is based on reason and universal justice. Based on the progressive dialectic, Star Trek conveys an inspirational vision—a society (*promised land*) where truth, justice, solidarity, fairness, and equality prevail. This vision is drawn from the secular philosophers/revolutionaries of Marx and Trotsky—with both being directly referenced in the sacred text.

Like all soothsaying texts, Star Trek is also a cautionary tale. It warns against false prophets: Nietzsche, Heidegger, Schmitt, and Strauss. To one degree or another, Star Trek engages the arguments of these naysayers (*heathens*). Nietzsche, the fountainhead of the anti-progressive dialectic crowd, expressly argued against the existence of the dialectic. Heidegger held that people's belief in the dialectic is a vain attempt to ease anxiety over death. Star Trek shows us that death is good, and that people actually fear eternal life (and the end of the dialectic) more than death itself. Moreover, death is central to the operation of the dialectic—with people desiring to make the most of their limited life by contributing to the progressive dialectic (see Chapter 3). Birth allows new people and ideas to enter the dialectic, and keep it anew (see Chapter 3). Additionally, the dialectic operates through biological evolution (a perpetual cycle of birth and death), with humans evolving toward a higher state of being (see Chapter 2). Seeking to replace the progressive dialectic with Schmitt's concept of the *other* will lead to political instability and risks destroying the planet. Finally, Strauss' prescription of returning society to a premodern theocracy is wrongheaded insofar as such an arrangement is politically dangerous and would serve to severely limit humanity's intellectual development. According to Star Trek, the pessimism and skepticism of Nietzsche *et al.* would lead humanity astray, and straight toward destruction.

CHAPTER 6

Star Trek and Language:
Dasein or Speculation?

Abstract Star Trek offers a fictional representation of a society/culture whose language is rooted in its *Dasein* (cultural practices, history, allegories, and mythical tales). Star Trek's fictional portrayal of such a language and society strongly suggests that it is implausible that such a society could exist, and, more importantly, advance into a technologically advanced civilization. Normatively speaking, such a language is undesirable because it would render a society isolated—simply unable to communicate in a meaningful, complex way with other societies/cultures. This would prevent meaningful speculation across different language groups.

Keywords Georg Hegel · The Absolute · Star Trek · Martin Heidegger

Richard Hanley, in *The Metaphysics of Star Trek*, takes up the question of the *Universal Translator*—the fictional device that allows humans to communicate with beings from other worlds. Hanley makes the point that if in fact humans are communicating with aliens through a translating device, shouldn't the mouthing of aliens reflect their own language and not that of spoken English.

Hanley's point is a valid one, but, just like in the case of whether or not Data is a person, the significance of the Universal Translator is not whether it is a credible technology, or one that is credibly portrayed. Instead, the Universal Translator reflects the idealism that everyone across the planet could one day easily speak to one another,[99] sharing

© The Author(s) 2017
G.A. Gonzalez, *The Absolute and Star Trek*,
DOI 10.1007/978-3-319-47794-7_6

their speculations about the *absolute*—thereby teaching each other the ways of actual justice, and helping to avoid *false infinities*.

An argument rooted in multi-culturalism, however, challenges this ideal. Those thinkers that embrace "Dasein"[100] as the basis of reason and knowledge hold language only allows the expression (the building) of culturally (geographically) rooted ideation. Put differently, language, reason, knowledge are largely culturally specific, and make much less sense across cultures.[101] Anthropological studies have found that certain types of words, and even particular logics, can be tied to specific cultures/geographies.[102] What would a language that is totally (mostly) tied to a specific culture actually look like? Is such a language possible, realistic, and/or consonant with modernity?

Star Trek offers a fictional representation of a society/culture whose language is rooted in its *Dasein* (cultural practices, history, allegories, and mythical tales). Star Trek's fictional portrayal of such a language and society strongly suggests that it is implausible that such a society could exist, and, more importantly, advance into a technologically advanced civilization. Normatively speaking, such a language is undesirable because it would render a society isolated—simply unable to communicate in a meaningful, complex way with other societies/cultures. This would prevent meaningful speculation across different language groups.

The *Children of Tama* (whose language is explicitly tied to their Dasein) are introduced in *The Next Generation* episode "Darmok" (1991). In contrast, the Federation is rooted in Hegelian concepts of language,[103] which makes possible Marxist conceptions of justice, social change, and world government (*internationalism*). The result is that the Federation is composed of heterodox peoples from across interstellar space, and based on a classless conception of equality—including the absence of gender and ethnic biases (*liberal humanism*).[104] One key aspect of the political unity in the Federation is precisely the ability of peoples from throughout interstellar space to communicate robust, complex ideas.

FEDERATION AND MODERNITY

World Government

World government in Star Trek ostensibly comes about because the nation-state system is a major political liability.[105] *Star Trek*, the original series, notes that humanity experienced a World War III in the 1990s—where tens-of-millions died. Spock, in "Bread and Circuses" (1968—original series), lists Earth's three world wars in the twentieth century—along with specific numbers of dead: "6 million" in World War I; "11 million" in World War II; and "37 million" in World War III. In "Space Seed" (1967—original series) the following is rendered: "The mid-1990s was the era of your last so-called world war." "The Eugenics War." As was the case in World Wars I and II, nation-states were the platforms for this fictional World War III. *Star Trek: The Next Generation* posits an episode with a world divided into two countries, which are beset with hostility, loathing, and deep suspicion toward one another.[106]

Star Trek's fictional history, where Earth's wars become progressively devastating, is consistent with Lenin's theory of international relations. Accruing to Marxist theory, Lenin argued that as capitalist economies became more and more unstable due to declining investment returns (as theorized by Marx) the world's nation-state system would de-stabilize and result in wars of greater and greater proportion.[107] Lenin wrote during World War I.[108] The creators of the original series worked in the aftermath of World War II and during the height of the Cold War. Thus, writing about a third world war occurring within a thirty-year frame was not much of a stretch. While this was a pessimistic view about humanity's inability to avoid another major war within a generation, Star Trek is optimistic about humanity's ability to overcome such devastating destruction and ultimately abolish one prime source of such devastation—the nation-state.

Present international politics point to the need for world government, as nation-states are continuing to serve as the basis for major military assaults. The advent of America's global hegemony (i.e., as the sole superpower)—with the collapse of the Soviet Union—has not initiated a peaceful/stable global regime—that is, the "end of history." Indeed, just as the Soviet Union was being dismantled, a major war took place in the heart of Eurasia. I am referring to the first Persian Gulf War—involving the Iraq invasion of Kuwait (1990) and the coalition of countries that rolled back the invasion (1991). The September 2001 hijacking of civilian airliners and their use as weapons against U.S. iconic structures (the New York Twin Towers and the Pentagon) brought about the U.S. invasion of Afghanistan—seemingly among the remotest of regions of the planet. In 2003, in defiance of international law, the United States organized and led "coalition of the willing" invaded and occupied Iraq. Libya, in 2011, had its government overthrown by another international coalition of nation-states. Globally devastating conflagrations are possible (if not likely). The United States and Russia, for instance, (the major nuclear weapon states) came into sharp opposition in 2008 over the country of Georgia. In 2014 events in the Ukraine once more heightened political/military tensions between nuclear-armed Great Powers (the United States, Russia, and the European Union). Writing in 2016, the U.S. and Russia are again in acute dispute. This time over the future of the government in Syria.

The optimism of world government inherent in Star Trek and by implication the *American Mind* is in part based on modern technology. With modern means of transportation and communication, the possibility of governing on a global scale appears absurdly obvious. This was even the case in the 1960s (*à la* Star Trek), before the current computer/internet revolution. The opportunity for world governance is so patent in a context where people are constantly traveling and communicating across the globe that darkly cast conspiracies of international government (i.e., the United Nations) are common fare amongst extremist nationalist groups—those most politically wed to their nation-states.[109] Extreme nationalism in opposition to global governance in the current epoch is consonant with the *Protocols of the Elders of Zion*—produced by the Russian Czar's secret police at the turn of the twentieth century—in which world government is cast as a dangerous cabal. The *Protocols of the Elders of Zion* can be perceived to be in direct response to *Angel of the Revolution*, written by H.G. Wells in 1892. Wells holds in this work of fiction that an Anglo-American-centered revolution defeats the forces of reaction and aristocracy worldwide—thereby establishing a global government founded on reason and justice.[110]

Regardless of whether world government is conceived as an objectionable impingement upon the sacred/venerable nation, or the institutional basis for peace and freedom, some type of world-wide regulatory regime is becoming more and more necessary. This is particularly evident with the climate change phenomenon. Collectively, the countries of the world are increasingly enhancing the heat trapping properties of the atmosphere.[111] With the dramatic decline of Arctic Ocean summer ice extent in 2012, the collapse of the Greenland ice sheet is a near to medium term likelihood. The result of all this would be catastrophic sea level rise and run-away global warming—as Arctic Ocean ice and Greenland ice anchor the planet's meteorology.[112] The nation-states of the planet have failed to negotiate a world-wide treaty to regulate/reduce greenhouse gas emissions.[113]

Meanwhile, such gases are being emitted at faster and faster rates, as the so-called developed nation-states are holding their massive and disproportionate global warming emissions steady and, at the same time, the *developing* nation-states (e.g., India and China) are accelerating their emissions.[114] Pointing to the inherent difficulties of protecting the environment in the context of multiple nation-states that have absolute sovereignty, the 1986 movie *Star Trek: The Voyage Home* explains that in the late twentieth century in spite of international agreements to prohibit whale hunting particular countries continue to sanction their killing.[115]

Related to the global warming phenomenon is the expanding human population.[116] Over the course of the twentieth century, and into the twenty-first, humanity has grown fourfold—from 1.6 billion to 7 billion—consuming increasing amounts of energy, food, and land.[117] Historian Matthew Connelly argues in his book *Fatal Misconception: The Struggle to Control World Population* that post–World War II population control efforts were marred by the perception and reality that such efforts were directed at specific countries and regions of the world.[118] The environmental movement of the late 1960s highlighted the threat of uncontrolled population growth.[119] "The Mark of Gideon" (1969), an original *Star Trek* series episode, conveys a planet where its population grows unchecked. This creates profound social and political problems. "The Conscience of the King" (1967—original series) references a dilemma in which a colony was too large for its food supply.

Therefore, Star Trek, especially the original series, draws attention to problems and issues that could be resolved through global government. Unlike narratives and political arguments that view world government as unworkable or inherently oppressive, Star Trek holds that establishing political sovereignty on a planetary-scale is a necessary step to achieve a peaceful and sustainable society.[120] World government is ostensibly more preferable than the current nation-state system, which is serving as the basis for persistent, and potentially expanding, military conflicts. Moreover, environmental issues, particularly the global warming crisis, do lead to the conclusion that world-wide regulatory regimes are needed if humanity and civilization are to survive.

Transportation and communication technologies are not the only reason that Star Trek is optimist about the possibilities and benefits of world government. American concepts of social/political assimilation (i.e., "America the Great Melting Pot") also inform Star Trek's optimism.

The "Great American Melting Pot"

The internationalist pretenses of Star Trek are a product of the American belief that all humans are capable of being assimilated into modern Western political culture—the highest manifestation of this culture presumably being the United States. Hence, the notion of the *American Melting Pot*, where people from throughout the world can come to the United States and be accepted. Viewing this from an optimist stance, the claim put forward (and embedded in Star Trek) is that modernity is transparent and accessible to all, as well as places few political burdens on individuals. Especially important, there are no religious obligations, nor any associated with ethnicity or lineage.[121] Captain Picard declares: "If there's one ideal the Federation holds most dear it's that all men, all [alien] races, can be united."[122]

Perhaps the core optimism conveyed in Star Trek is the ability of people from all ethnic backgrounds (and from other planets) to live peacefully together and fruitfully collaborate. During a *Next Generation* 1990 episode, a visiting alien is very impressed with the highly diverse background of the Enterprise crew: "These people ... they're all so different from one another ... yet they work together freely." "Truly remarkable."[123] Operating through reason, science, and a common language (English), humans virtually throughout the Star Trek series and movies get along with little rancor or divisiveness. Star Trek is also distinctive for the intelligence and maturity of humans (and that of their fictional alien partners). A particular signature feature of Star Trek is the ability of its characters to maneuver complex (fictional) technologies. This is indicative of the putative transparency and accessibility of reason, science, and technology. It is also reflective of the belief that virtually every human has the mental capability to attain very high levels of knowledge, emotional maturity, and technical proficiency.

According to Star Trek this plateau of human development is the result of revolutionary processes—as explained in Chapter 4. Therefore, human advancement is not simply the result of "natural" progression, but instead it is in part the result of conceptualizing America as a continuing project of "justice." Hence, if America is exceptional, it is because it was founded on abstract principles of justice. Ideally, people from any place or ethnic background can join this project. Thus, Lafayette, a Frenchmen, and Thomas Paine, a recently arrived Scotsman, could take prominent roles in the American Revolution—a fight against empire and aristocracy.[124] Later, in the nineteenth century, newly arrived immigrants from Ireland,

Germany, etc. (and African-Americans) would join together to militarily defeat the Southern slave owning class in the American Civil War.[125] *Star Trek* in "City on the Edge of Forever" (1967—original series) takes up the U.S. entrance into World War II—where soldiers with greatly varying ethnic backgrounds served under the American banner.

Star Trek, therefore, takes the "Great American Melting Pot" idea to its logical conclusion—namely, that modernity; science; reason can serve as the basis for a peaceful; highly productive; and thriving world. Star Trek is optimistic insofar as arguing that as global society accepts modernity; reason; science (i.e., the Enlightenment) humans will collectively achieve a higher plane of intelligence; knowledge; and emotional immaturity. (An optimism shared by Marx: in "communist society...the all-round development of the individual" will be achieved.[126])

Taking this thinking further, Star Trek posits the argument that a stable, ethical society can only be based on a classless society founded on reason and free of gender and ethnic biases (more specifically, internationalism/world government). Nevertheless, Star Trek acknowledges and conveys the argument against global government and universal communication. The *Children of Tama* challenges the internationalism that the Federation is predicated upon, as they are a group/ethnicity whose language is based explicitly on its *Dasein*. The *Children of Tama* suggest that it is foolhardy to think that all the peoples of the world could be voluntarily politically united, as language (which is rooted in Dasein) would make such voluntary unity impossible. In the end, the Star Trek portrayal of the Children of Tama suggests that such societies are not possible, and could certainly never be fully modern or technologically advanced. Thus, Star Trek demonstrates that the Dasein notion of language (on the whole) is empirically invalid.[127] Additionally, such languages are normatively undesirable insofar as they would isolate their societies.

The Children of Tama

While the Children of Tama are space faring and very technologically advanced, they are unable to communicate to the Federation. "Federation vessels have encountered Tamarian ships seven times over the past one hundred years. Each meeting went without incident, however formal relations were not established because communication was not possible." The episode of "Darmok" revolves around an effort on the part of Tamarians to again communicate with the Federation, and specifically with the Enterprise crew. The following is the first message from the Tamarian ship: "Rai and Jiri at Lungha. Rai of Lowani. Lowani under two moons. Jiri of Ubaya. Ubaya of crossed roads at Lungha. Lungha, her sky grey. Rai and Jiri at Lungha." Their language can be translated, but much of it is proper names, which have no meaning whatsoever for the Enterprise crew. We subsequently learn that the Tamarians "communicate through narrative imagery by reference to the individuals and places which appear in their mytho-historical accounts." "Imagery is everything to the Tamarians. It embodies their emotional states, their very thought processes. It's how they communicate, and it's how they think." To translate the Tarmarian language it requires the mastering of their Dasein:

> It is necessary for us to learn the narrative from which the Tamarians are drawing their imagery.
> The situation is analogous to understanding the grammar of a language but none of the vocabulary.
> If I didn't know who Juliet was or what she was doing on that balcony, the image alone wouldn't have any meaning.

Just like one has to understand the human *Dasein* (i.e., Shakespeare) to access the meaning of Juliet on the balcony ("romance"), Federation personnel would have to immerse themselves in the Tamarians' Dasein to grasp their language.

On the face of it, a language based on imagery drawn from "mytho-historical accounts" is impossible. How does one achieve society-wide consensus on what mytho-historical account represents every rudimentary observation? For instance, how would someone say "see dog run" based on mytho-historical accounts? More dauntingly, how do you incorporate new knowledge, technologies, and experiences into a language predicated on mytho-historical accounts? For example, how does one meaningfully, robustly treat quantum mechanics? It appears to be impossible, and certainly impractical.

The Tamarian plan to bridge the communication gap between themselves and the Federation drew on a parable: "Darmok and Jalad, the beast of Tanagra. They arrived separately. They struggled together against a common foe, the beast at Tanagra. Darmok and Jalad at Tanagra." Picard to the Tarmarian ship captain: "You hoped this would happen, didn't you? You knew there was a dangerous creature on this planet and you knew from the tale of Darmok that a danger shared might sometimes bring two people together. Darmok and Jalad at

Tanagra. You and me, here, at El-Adrel." Such simplistic, clunky (imprecise) concepts can hardly be the basis of a modern, sophisticated society.

Perhaps more damning, the Child of Tama cannot communicate with others. Thus, in spite of the best efforts of the Taramins and the Enterprise, the two are unable to have a meeting of the minds. Presumably, the Taramins would be unable to share ideas with few, if any, societies.

CONCLUSION

The very idea of Federation is that peoples from throughout interstellar space can meaningfully unite and form a single polity: "The Federation is made up of over a hundred planets *who have allied themselves* for mutual scientific, cultural and defensive benefits" ("Battle Lines" 1993—Deep Space Nine). "The Federation consists of over one hundred and fifty different worlds *who have agreed to share their knowledge and resources in peaceful cooperation*" ("Innocence" 1996—*Voyager*). Kirk, speaking of the founders of the Federation: "They were humanitarians and statesmen, and they had a dream. A dream that became a reality and spread throughout the stars, a dream that made Mister Spock and me brothers" ("Whom the Gods Destroy" 1969—original series). Star Trek suggests that the basis of such unity is justice as defined by a classless society (á la Karl Marx), free of gender and ethnic biases *(liberal humanism)*.

Proponents of Dasein argue that such universal unity as represented in Federation is unworkable, because societies in fact base themselves on their history, culture, tradition, and what amount to idiosyncratic language.[128] The Star Trek episode of "Darmok" takes up this notion of language as reflective of peoples' culture, myths, and history. Notwithstanding the fictional setup of the episode (whereby the Taramins are cast as technologically advanced), the Children of Tama appear as incapable of the kind of sophisticated thinking required to deploy modernism (and ultimately space travel). This is precisely because their thinking and language are rooted in the past and operates purely on the basis of culturally based allegories and metaphors.

Moreover, such a language would serve to isolate the Taramins and prevent them from substantively interacting (speculating) with peoples from outside their society. In the end, we have to conclude that notions of culturally based language, as posited by champions of Dasein, are simply false, as, unlike the Children of Tama, all humans can learn each other's languages, and, can, on the whole, fruitfully apply these languages in any cultural context or geography.

CHAPTER 7

Star Trek: Prejudice versus Universal Rationality

Abstract Precisely because Star Trek's creators seek to sensitively portray and maneuver around Klingon prejudices, through this franchise the viewer can see that a polity based on prejudices is undesirable—whereas one informed by reason (Marxism) is inspirational. More specifically, the Star Trek text indicates that societies based on prejudices are subject to racism/xenophobia, as well as political stagnation/instability. In contrast, societies based on reason (i.e., the Federation) are politically/socially vibrant and thrive.

Keywords Georg Hegel · The Absolute · Star Trek · Martin Heidegger

Adam Adatto Sandel, in *The Place of Prejudice*, makes a provocative argument on behalf of prejudice in politics. Sandel (drawing heavily on Heidegger) asserts that knowledge situated in specific cultures is needed if reason can be fully/meaningfully applied and be consonant with liberty: "prejudices can be illuminating and also consistent with freedom."[129] Unsurprisingly, Sandel takes issue with reason (as broadly understood): "detached judgement as itself a prejudice—an aspiration shaped by a questionable tradition of thought."[130] Thus, there are types of knowledge that are only accessible to those that have lived/experienced particular cultures. Moreover, reason can only be effective and consistent with freedom if the person doing the reasoning is sensitive to knowledge claims

G.A. Gonzalez, *The Absolute and Star Trek*,
DOI 10.1007/978-3-319-47794-7_7

(*prejudices*) made by those intimately familiar with specific cultures. Presumably, claims about universal human rights or universal fairness/ justice are *a priori* misguided—as ideas (*prejudices*) about rights and justice will vary to at least some degree from culture to culture.

The Star Trek franchise (especially beginning with *The Next Generation*) offers an excellent (obviously fictional) opportunity to juxtapose Sandel's politics of *prejudice* with a politics of universal *reason*. The Federation is a polity predicated on *reason*, whereas the Klingon Empire is founded on *prejudice*. Therefore, while the Federation is evidently a product of the Enlightenment (more specifically Marxism), the Klingons' society and politics are explicitly based on tradition and cultural identity ("Dasein"[131]).

Precisely because Star Trek's creators seek to sensitively portray and maneuver around Klingon prejudices, through this franchise the viewer can see that a polity based on prejudices is undesirable—whereas one informed by reason (Marxism) is inspirational. More specifically, the Star Trek text indicates that societies based on prejudices are subject to racism/ xenophobia, as well as political stagnation/instability. In contrast, societies based on reason (i.e., the Federation) are politically/socially vibrant and thrive.

With humanity basing itself on a "philosophy of self-enhancement" (see Chapter 4), humans come to lead the Federation, and, most importantly, its expansion is predicated on voluntary merger/union. Indicative of seemingly how the social justice politics (broadly conceived—i.e., *universalism*) of the Federation transcends all ethnic, religious (species) divisions, during a *Next Generation* 1990 episode, a visiting alien is very impressed with the highly diverse background of the Enterprise crew: "These people...they're all so different from one another...yet they work together freely." "Truly remarkable" ("Transfigurations").

Star Trek posits the argument that a stable, ethical society can only be based on a classless society based on modernism—one that is free of gender and ethnic biases (see Chapter 4). Star Trek, however, does offer a society (the Klingons) based on Heidegger's concept of *Dasein*— knowledge derived literally from "Being-There."

THE KLINGON DASEIN

Unlike the Federation, which is based on the universal ideas of equality, fairness, and just treatment, Klingons are traditionalists. Traditionalist societies (those based on Dasein) tend to be patriarchies, as is Klingon society—with women prohibited from sitting on the Klingon's supreme political body, the *High Council*; political decisions for the family/clan are made by the eldest male; and the crimes of fathers implicate their sons ("Sins of the Father" 1990, "Reunion" 1990 and "Redemption" 1991— all *Next Generation* episodes).

The fictional Klingons base their polity on ethnic identity—hence, the name of their polity, the *Klingon* Empire. (Klingons in fact are not a different species from humans, as Klingon-human couplings can result in offspring.)[132] Klingons look to their past and religion (i.e., Dasein) to shape and legitimatize their politics. The episode "Rightful Heir" (1993—*Next Generation*) focuses on the figure of Kahless, who is credited with founding the Klingon state. According to Klingon theology, Kahless "united" the Klingons, gave them "honor and strength," and "promised to return one day and lead us again." Kahless is described as a prophet-like figure in the following: "To believe in Kahless and his teachings...and to become truly Klingon." Kahless is cloned from ancient DNA material, and the Kahless clone is made head of the state for the Klingon Empire.

Pointing to the traditionalism of the Klingons, ancient (i.e., traditional) rituals serve as an important part of their society.[133] As noted by a Klingon, "If someone wishes to join us [to marry into a Klingon family], they must honor our traditions" ("You Are Cordially Invited" 1997— *Deep Space Nine*). Significantly, instead of using modern (democratic and transparent) means of selecting a head of government, the Klingons employ the "rite of succession"—an oblique ritual/tradition—to select their political leader. In this rite, the "Arbiter of Succession" (with no clear criteria) decides who are the "strongest challengers" to vie for the Chancellorship ("Reunion" 1990). One presumes that the Arbiter of Succession has intimate knowledge of the Klingon's Dasein, which allows him to make a well "reasoned" decision.

Star Trek makes specific reference to the Klingon's *Dasein*, and makes allowances for it. When Worf becomes paralyzed, he decides to commit suicide ("Ethics" 1992—*Next Generation*). Picard supports his decision. Enterprise's First Officer William Riker rejects Worf's desire to commit suicide, holding that his paralysis "doesn't mean his life is over." Picard disagrees, expressly pointing to the Klingon Dasein (even chiding Riker for applying the putatively human *Dasein* to Worf [a Klingon]): "That's a very human perspective, Will. For a Klingon in Worf's position, his life is over." Picard continues: "You or I could learn to live with that disability, but not Worf. His life ended when those containers fell on him. We don't have to agree with it, we don't have to understand it, but we do have to respect his beliefs." In the end, Picard encourages Riker to honor Worf's request to help him commit suicide: "Klingons choose their friends with great care. If he didn't know he could count on you, he never would have asked."

Even as the Klingon polity (one based as Dasein) is portrayed with sympathy (respect) by Star Trek's creators, they nevertheless point to the inherent limitations and pitfalls of basing a society on *prejudices*. Perhaps the worst aspect of a world permanently cleaved into different Daseins is the xenophobia and racism that would seemingly be forever part of global politics. When the figure of Kahless appears (in "Rightful Heir"), the Klingons present share in a moment of pride (and exclusion) in their ethnic identity, chanting "We are Klingons. We are Klingons. We are Klingons. We are Klingons. We are Klingons. We are Klingons." The xenophobia of traditionalism/Dasein is evident when Worf is chided for bringing "*outsiders* [i.e., humans] to our Great Hall" ("Sins of the Father" 1990). In another instance, one Klingon is opposed to another Klingon marrying a non-Klingon: "She believes that by bringing aliens into our families we risk losing our identity as Klingons." This is acknowledged as "a prejudiced, xenophobic view" ("You Are Cordially Invited").

The xenophobia (even racism) inherent in the Dasein concept posited by Heidegger is particularly evident in *The Next Generation* episode "Birthright" (1993). The action centers on a prison camp established by the Romulans over 20 years earlier to house a group of Klingons who could not return home. They were stigmatized by the fact that they were taken prisoner—Klingons are expected to fight to the death or commit suicide if captured. As an act of kindness, and at great sacrifice, a Romulan officer agrees to oversee the camp—otherwise the captured Klingons would be executed. Worf—whose father was falsely rumored to be at the camp—discovers it. He objects to an arrangement whereby Klingons live as prisoners of the Romulans—even though they are treated well; have complete freedom on the planet they reside on; have given birth to children; and share a strong sense of community. Worf, nevertheless, tells the Romulan camp commander (Tokath) that "you robbed the Klingons of who they were. *You dishonored them.*" Tokath, pointing to the irrationality of Worf's position, retorts: "By not slitting their throats when we found them unconscious?" Worf explicitly points to the Klingon

Dasein to justify his position: "I do not expect you to understand. *You are a Romulan.*" Hence, there is something *particular* about Klingons, and it is inscrutable to a Romulan—who has no contact with Klingon culture. Tokath explains "we've put aside the old hatreds. Here, Romulans and Klingons live in peace." Worf is unmoved (again claiming special knowledge [Dasein] about Klingons): "Do not deceive yourself. These people are not happy here. I see the sadness in their eyes."

Worf adopts an openly hateful attitude when he comes to discover that a woman (Ba'el) he is romantically interested in is an offspring of one of the Klingon prisoners and a Romulan. Worf is kissing Ba'el, draws back her hair and sees her pointed ears (characteristic of Romulans). Outraged, Worf exclaims "*You are Romulan!*" Unabashed in his racism, he asks with a tone of disgust: *"How could your mother mate with a Romulan?"* He declares *"it is an obscenity!"* Fully venting his racism, Worf tells Ba'el: "Romulans are *treacherous, deceitful.* They are without honor." Ba'el: "My father is a good man. He is kind, and generous. There is nothing dishonorable about him."

Perhaps the darkest manifestation of Dasein in the Star Trek franchise occurs in the *Enterprise* episode "Cogenitor" (2003). The Enterprise crew befriends a ship from an alien species heretofore unknown to humans— *Vissians.* Vissians have a third sex—a *cogenitor*, who is needed for procreation. Cogenitors compose 3 percent of the population, and are treated like slaves. So while they have the same cognitive abilities as the rest of their species, cogenitors are not allowed to read, learn, and are perpetually confined to quarters. One of the Enterprise crew (Charles "Trip" Tucker) intervenes to help the cogenitor on the alien ship—teaching it to read and encouraging it to expand its horizons. The cogenitor asks Captain Jonathan Archer of Enterprise for asylum—as in its society the cogenitor will never be given the opportunity to lead a normal life. In seeking to justify their treatment of cogenitors, one of the Vissians invokes the notion of Dasein: "You have no right to judge us. You know nothing about our culture." In the end, Archer refuses the cogenitor asylum, and it subsequently commits suicide. Archer holds Tucker responsible for the cogenitor's death, arguing that he should not have defied the Dasein of the Vissians. Archer goes further and asserts that the concept of human rights only applies to humans: "You knew you had no business interfering with those people, but you just couldn't let it alone. You thought you were doing the right thing. I might agree if this was Florida, or Singapore, but it's not, is it."

One criticism of Heidegger's idea that polities are/should be based on Dasein is that such societies stagnate. Put differently, societies that value Dasein are *repetitive*: "The individual is ready to accept his heritage...This stance toward one's historical past is its 'repetition'."[134] As a prominent Klingon stated, "We don't embrace other cultures" ("You Are Cordially Invited"). This is in contrast to the Federation's *telos*—predicated on incorporating new knowledge, cultures, norms, etc. Captain Picard declares: "If there's one ideal the Federation holds most dear it's that all men, all [alien] races, can be united" (*Star Trek: Nemesis* 2002). Thus, whereas the Federation is based on a *telos* of reason, its political stability is never in question. In *The Next Generation* episode "Transfigurations" (1990) the argument is seemingly made that humanity through its *telos* is moving toward a higher form of being (see Chapter 2).

Conversely, the Klingons grapple with the issue of how to maintain the Empire's political/social vigor. Klingons point to warfare as a way to normatively energize the Empire. This argument is made in the episode "Heart of Glory" (1988—*Next Generation*). The plot centers on two Klingons who hold that the peace with the Federation is undermining Klingon values (Dasein): "Brother, this peace, this alliance, is like a living death to warriors like us." "A peace that makes the Klingon heart that beats in my chest wither and die." The claim here is that violence/conquest is central to the Klingon Dasein (the Empire's leaders have "traded our birthright so they could die in their sleep.") Worf finds himself drawn to the dissidents' arguments. Picard acknowledges to Worf: "I am not unmindful of the mixed feelings you must have about this incident." The point is even made that desire for war/violence is rooted in Klingon's genes: the steadfastly objective Data notes that "there is, of course, a genetic predisposition toward hostility among all Klingons" ("The Icarus Factor" 1989—*Next Generation*).

The political decay/atrophying of the Klingon Empire is a central theme in "Rightful Heir." In cloning Kahless and trying to pass him off as the actual Kahless resurrected, the perpetrators justify their actions by pointing to the seeming political ennui afflicting the Empire: Kahless "is needed by our people. You know better than anyone the corruption and dishonor that has destroyed the Empire. They need him." Worf agrees with this assessment: "Our people are becoming decadent and corrupt. They need moral leadership. Kahless can be that leader, as Emperor."

CONCLUSION

The Star Trek broadcast franchise (especially beginning with *Next Generation*) offers a fascinating and elucidating juxtaposition between a society based on reason—more specifically, Trotskite Marxism—and one based on Dasein. The history of Earth is cast as a series of progressive revolutions, resulting in the human race leading an interstellar institution of heterodox peoples (the Federation) (see Chapter 4). The indication is made that this *telos* will result in humanity achieving a higher plane of existence (see Chapter 2). The Klingons, in contrast, are politically based on *Dasein*—their specific history, traditions, and religious beliefs. Whereas the Federation seemingly looks to the future for legitimacy (i.e., presumably the degree to which the *telos* is advanced), the Klingons look to the past—seeking to follow/emulate "great" figures from history (e.g., Kahless).

Noted at the beginning of this discussion, Adam Adatto Sandel holds that *prejudice* in politics can lead to optimal outcomes—maximizing the effectiveness of reason and enhancing freedom. Moreover, he implies that universal (*detached*) reason is a dubious enterprise, essentially unworkable outside of Dasein. Taking Star Trek as a political theory text, it leads to diametrically opposite conclusions. Polities based on universal reason (the Federation) are inclusive, vibrant, and just, whereas those predicated on Dasein (the Klingon Empire) are xenophobic, hostile, and unstable/corrupt. Additionally, with the *Enterprise* episode "Cogenitor" we see the idea of Dasein invoked to justify slavery. What is particularly significant about Star Trek's conclusions via Dasein is that the concept is taken seriously and thoughtfully applied—embraced by leading characters (Captains Picard and Archer). This makes its treatment of Dasein all the more powerful and relevant.

CHAPTER 8

Star Trek: Voyager: Pragmatism and Neo-Pragmatism as False Infinities

Abstract The creators of Star Trek dedicated virtually an entire series (*Voyager*) to show how pragmatism and neo-pragmatism lead to undesirable/unstable/catastrophic outcomes. Conversely, the series depicts how ethics and principles are key to (yes!) achieving success in the face of dire/difficult circumstances.

Keywords Georg Hegel · The Absolute · Star Trek

The Star Trek franchise indicates that *pragmatism* and *neo-pragmatism* represent *false infinities*. In some respects the arch-nemesis of speculation as a philosophical method is pragmatism.[135] But pragmatism should not be confused for practicality—the rejection of abstract reasoning in favor of direct action to resolve/address specific/immediate circumstances. Unlike practicality (and instrumental reason), pragmatism is predicated on a metaphysics—specifically, that societal stability exists outside of justice or other ethical considerations. Thus, pragmatists do speculate about how to maintain societal stability. Where pragmatists and Hegel/Marx part ways is over ethics and the very idea of justice. While those working in the Hegelian tradition argue that the *absolute* (and by implication societal stability) operates through justice and ethics,[136] American pragmatists have historically argued that, broadly speaking, we should avoid holding hard and fast to ethics or political principles—lest societal stability be threatened. Harvard historian Louis Menand points out that the core of *pragmatism* is "the belief that ideas [ethics, morality] should never become ideologies"—which early pragmatists saw as the cause of the American Civil War.[137]

The most trenchant critique of pragmatism is arguably made in the original series episode "Bread and Circuses" (1968), where the argument is made that an overriding emphasis on societal stability would result in the persistence of slavery worldwide. The Enterprise crew comes upon a planet that is virtually identical to mid-20th Earth (America); except on this world the Roman Empire never collapsed and, instead, spans the entire planet. "A world ruled by emperors who can trace their line back 2000 years to their own Julius and Augustus Caesars." The result is that slavery continues—in part because the slave system was reformed to maintain its stability: "Long ago, there were [slave] rebellions" but "with each century, the slaves acquired more rights under the law. They received rights to medicine, the right to government payments in their old age, and they slowly learned to be content." Spock: "Slavery evolving into an institution with guaranteed medical payments, old-age pensions." In defending this society, one of the characters explains: "This is an ordered world, a conservative world based on time-honored Roman strengths and virtues. . . . There's been no war here for over 400 years." "Could your land of that same era make that same boast?", he asks of the Enterprise landing party (specifically Kirk and McCoy). Explaining why Federation citizens who had come upon this Rome-like world could not be allowed to leave (thereby having the opportunity to tell others of its existence): "I think you can see why they don't want to have their *stability* contaminated by dangerous ideas of other ways and places"—that is, *ideologies* of freedom, democracy, equality, etc., that could be politically destabilizing. Spock, in response, opines: "given a conservative empire, quite understandable."

INTERSUBJECTIVE AGREEMENT (NEO-PRAGMATISM)

American philosopher, Richard Rorty, writing in the early 1980s, in fashioning *neo-pragmatism* argues that societies are based on *intersubjective agreement*.[138] Thus, what is required for societal stability is enough consensus on a set of ideas—any set of ideas. Hence, what matters is consensus, and not the ideas themselves. Presumably, when there is not enough intersubjective consensus/agreement, then social/political breakdown occurs.

Over ten years before Rorty published his path-breaking notion of *intersubjective agreement*, the original series Star Trek episode "Mirror,

Mirror" (1967) aired. Members of the Enterprise crew (including Kirk and McCoy), through a technical glitch, are beamed to an alternate universe. The Enterprise (including Spock) exists in this alternate universe, but instead of the Federation the political authority is the "Empire"—where "behavior and discipline" is "brutal, savage." Captain Kirk (from the Federation) refuses to carry out the order to destroy a planet that refuses to comply with the Empire. Spock (sporting a mustache and goatee) notes to Kirk: "No one will question the assassination of a captain who has disobeyed prime orders of the Empire." Kirk: "I command an Enterprise where officers apparently employ private henchmen among the crew, where assassination of superiors is a common means of advancing in rank." McCoy asks, "What kind of people are we in this universe?":

Kirk:	Let's find out
Kirk (to the ship's computer):	Read out official record of current command.
Computer:	Captain James T. Kirk succeeded to command I.S.S. Enterprise through assassination of Captain Christopher Pike. First action—suppression of Gorlan uprising through destruction of rebel home planet. Second action—execution of 5,000 colonists on Vega 9 . . .
Kirk (interrupting the computer):	Cancel
McCoy:	Now we know

The Captain Jonathan Archer from the alternative universe declares that "Great men are not peacemakers. Great men are conquerors" ("In a Mirror, Darkly" 2005—*Enterprise*). The implication of "Mirror, Mirror" (and "In a Mirror, Darkly") is irrespective of their value system—whether "Empire" or "Federation"—humans' can create and lead a vast interstellar political formation. Technological progress and political stability would essentially be the same.

The *intersubjective agreement* argument in "Mirror, Mirror" is brought into sharper relief in *Deep Space Nine*, where the alternate universe is revisited a century later.[139] We learn that Kirk's time in the alternate universe had a profound impact. "On my side, Kirk is one of the most famous names in our history." In "Mirror, Mirror" Kirk apprized Spock of a weapon ("the Tantalus field"). From one's quarters a person could zero in on victims and with the push of a button make them disappear. This presages U.S. drone technology, where operators in an air conditioned facility in Nevada guide small airplanes (drones) flying over remote regions of the world, and with the push of a button fire missiles on unsuspecting individuals from 50,000 feet.[140] Kirk counseled Spock to use such technology to profoundly change the Empire, and base it on the values of the Federation. When Spock, however, disrupts the *intersubjective agreement* that was the basis of the Empire, it collapses:

> Almost a century ago, a Terran starship Captain named James Kirk accidentally exchanged places with his counterpart from your side due to a transporter accident. Our Terrans were barbarians then, but their Empire was strong. While your Kirk was on this side, he met a Vulcan named Spock and somehow had a profound influence on him. Afterwards, Spock rose to commander in chief of the Empire by preaching reforms, disarmament, peace. It was a remarkable turnabout for his people. Unfortunately for them, when Spock had completed all these reforms, his empire was no longer in any position to defend itself against us.

The end result is that the Earth is conquered and occupied.

The creators of Star Trek dedicated virtually an entire series (*Voyager*) to showing how pragmatism and neo-pragmatism lead to undesirable/unstable/catastrophic outcomes. Conversely, the series depicts how ethics and principles are key to (*yes!*) achieving success in the face of dire/difficult circumstances.

THE ETHICS OF STAR TREK

Star Trek: Voyager represents a metaphor of being lost in the so-called Third World.[141] Through this metaphor, *Voyager* focuses on *pragmatism* and *neo-pragmatism*. The show begins when the star ship Voyager is transported 70,000 light years from Federation space. It is estimated that to get back to Earth it would take Voyager seventy-five years using the propulsion means at its disposal. During the course of its daunting effort to traverse this massive expanse of space, the Voyager crew encounters numerous situations fraught with moral/ethnic quandaries. In facing these quandaries/dilemmas the Voyager crew has to decide whether to be expeditious (i.e., pragmatic) in trying to get home, or to prioritize their ethical/moral principles (thereby endangering themselves and their chances of getting home). The strength of the show, in my estimation, is that the Voyager crew consistently chose to be ethical even in the face of death (or remaining stranded). Moreover, certain villains in the Voyager series are dastardly precisely because they prioritize *pragmatism* over principle.

Anti-*Pragmatism*

The anti-*pragmatism* of *Voyager* starts with its first episode ("The Caretaker" 1995), and the setting of the show's premise. Voyager and her crew are transported into the *Delta Quadrant* of the galaxy. (The Federation is in the *Alpha Quadrant.*) Voyager was brought to this part of space by a creature known as the "Caretaker." The Caretaker is dying, and he is seeking to mate with someone. Why the Caretaker finds it particularly imperative to have an offspring is because he is manning an "Array" in space that sustains/protects a species known as the *Ocampa*. An offspring would presumably continue to operate the array. We learn that the Caretaker had brought a number of species from throughout the galaxy in an effort to find a suitable mate.

The Caretaker is in his last moments of life, and failing to have a child, is undertaking an effort to sure up the Ocampa's defenses to prevent the *Kazon*—a hostile race—from overrunning Ocampa society. Upon the Caretaker's death, the Kazon make Voyager an offer: they would cease their attack against Voyager (allowing it to use the array to return home) and the Kazon could then use the array to invade the Ocampans. Thus, from the virtual inception of the show, the Voyager crew face a vexing dilemma: make peace with Kazon at the expense of the Ocampa (thereby going home) or destroy the array to protect the Ocampa—hence, becoming stranded in a remote part of space. The Voyager crew destroys the array.

Outside of the series pilot, three Voyager episodes stand out for the ethical/moral/principled behavior of the crew—in an otherwise demoralizing and physically isolated circumstance (seventy five years from home): "False Profits" (1996), "Dreadnought" (1996), and "The Void" (2001). In "False Profits" Voyager comes across a "worm hole" that leads directly to the Alpha Quadrant (i.e., Federation space). Thus, by entering this worm hole the Voyager crew would instantaneously be home. But before they enter this portal the Voyager crew discovers that a planet proximate to it is being exploited by a pair of Ferengis. The Ferengis presence on the planet relates back to *The Next Generation* ("The Price" 1989). The star ship Enterprise was heading a Federation delegation bidding on the rights to a worm hole that linked the Alpha and Delta Quadrant—the worm hole that Voyager can now use to get home. In preparation for the bidding, shuttle craft from both the Enterprise and a Ferengi ship passed through the worm hole to investigate this phenomenon. The Enterprise crew, upon reaching the Delta Quadrant side of the worm hole, conclude that the worm hole is unstable and that the aperture on the Delta Quadrant side will randomly move—thereby threatening to strand anyone on that side of the worm hole. The crew of the Enterprise shuttle warn that the worm hole aperture is about to shift to some unknown location, but the Ferengi refuse to listen. So while the Enterprise shuttle craft safely returns to the Alpha Quadrant, the Ferengi do not.

In *Voyager* we learn that the two Ferengi ("Arridor" and "Kol") since getting stranded in the Delta Quadrant made their way to a nearby planet, where they were able to exploit the native population's religious beliefs to attain a dominant political position. (The Ferengis are recognized as "The Holy Sages.") ("It seems the people have a myth, an epic poem called the 'Song of the Sages', which predicts the arrival of two demigods from the sky, the sages, who would rule over the people as benevolent protectors.") Fergenis, as a species, elevate capitalist ideology to a religion (with their heaven being known as the Divine Treasury, and only those with sufficient profit can enter). As part of their capitalist religion/ideology, Fergeni have what are known as the "Rules of Acquisition"—a set of nostrums that Ferengis can putatively rely on in their profit-making endeavors: for example, "Exploitation begins at home"; "Expand or die"; "A wise man can hear profit in the wind." Therefore, when the native population of the Delta Quadrant planet believe the Ferengis to be deities the Ferengis establish a regime that allows them to economically exploit the planet. "False Profits" is an extension of the Star Trek franchise's ongoing criticism of capitalism/ neoliberalism (see Chapter 4). Before the arrival of the Ferengis the native population (we are told) was "flourishing." Under the Ferengis profit-making regime Arridor and Kol become very wealthy, and at the same time poverty proliferates among the native population. ("The two Ferengi live in a palatial temple, while the people are lucky to have a roof over their heads.")

The Voyager crew feel that they have a moral responsibility to remove the Fergenis from the planet—thereby ending the profit prioritizing government they have created. ("The Federation did host the negotiations. And if it were not for those negotiations, the Ferengi would not be here. So one could say, without being unreasonable I think, that the Federation is partially responsible for what's happened, and therefore, duty bound to correct the situation.") Thus, instead of simply going through the worm hole and immediately going home, the Voyager crew seek to end the Ferengis' rule in an orderly fashion—in a way consistent with the society's theology. Growing resentful of the Ferengis and their rule, elements of the native population help draw on aspects of their religion to expel the Ferengis. Untrustworthy as ever, in the final instance the Ferengis use their space ship to try to return to the planet. Their shenanigans sends them through the worm hole (destabilizing it)—leaving Voyager stranded.

"Dreadnought" is similar to "False Profits" insofar events in the distant Alpha Quadrant initiate the action. *Dreadnought* is a massive missile that is roaming through space in the Delta Quadrant. The missile was programmed and launched in the Alpha Quadrant by Voyager's chief engineer, B'elenna Torres. This is when she was a member of the *Maquis*—an insurgent movement directed mostly at the Cardassian Alliance, which, according to the Maquis, brutalize their subject peoples. (In the series pilot, a Maquis ship and Voyager were pulled to the Delta Quadrant together. Much of *Star Trek: Voyager* involves the process whereby the maquis are incorporated into the Voyager crew—including its command structure [hence, Torres becoming Voyager's chief engineer].) The Dreadnought was wantonly launched by Torres into Cardassian space, and ended up in the Delta Quadrant. Torres, now a member of the Voyager crew, repents for unleashing Dreadnought, and undertakes great risks to disarm this weapon of mass destruction. Hence, Torres' membership in the Voyager crew, and Captain Kathryn Janeway serving as her mentor, develops Torres' moral sensibilities and leads her to the conclusion that blindly launching a weapon of such destructive capacity is ethically/morally wrong—regardless of the circumstance. What is particularly germane for a discussion involving *pragmatism* is the fact that (in case Torres failed to disarm the missile) Voyager is ready to throw itself in the way of Dreadnought to prevent it from devastating a planet it had locked in on.

Janeway:	I'm prepared to use this ship to detonate the warhead before the missile reaches you.
	Use your ship? To collide with it?
Janeway:	Something like that.
	You would sacrifice yourselves to benefit a people you didn't even know two days ago?
Janeway:	To save two million lives? That's not a hard decision.

Hence, Voyager does not take the expedient position that they (nor the Federation) are responsible for Dreadnought. Instead, the Voyager crew is ready to sacrifice itself for moral/ethical reasons.

Voyager episode "The Void" makes an explicit claim of the importance of operating on foundational principles—rejecting *pragmatism.*[142] Voyager is trapped in a "void" in space (where there is no "matter of any kind"). Other ships trapped in the void have taken up the practice of attacking/raiding other trapped ships for supplies as a means of surviving. ("There are more than one hundred fifty ships within scanning range but I'm only detecting life signs on twenty nine of them.")

A captain from one of the other stranded ships advises Voyager to abandon her ethical principles in the Void: "Wait a few weeks until your resources start to run out. Morality won't keep your life support systems running." Implying she would die for her principles, Captain Janeway responds: "I'm sorry, General. There are some compromises I won't make."

Nonetheless, members of Voyager's crew, in retrieving stolen supplies, suggest that they take supplies from another ship that never belonged to them. Janeway, nevertheless, refuses to act unethically—even while acknowledging other ship captains in the void would not limit themselves by ethical considerations.

> I'm detecting large quantities of food on his supply deck.
> Maybe we should take it while we have the chance.

> *Captain Janeway:*   Is it ours?
>   No, but our own reserves are running out.
>   Valen (the commander of the ship in question)
>   wouldn't hesitate to take it from us.
> *Captain Janeway:*   No, he wouldn't. We've got what's ours. Reverse
>   course.

After Captain Janeway refused to take other than what was taken from Voyager, her most senior officers (Tuvok and Chakotay) approach her about this decision.

> *Chakotay:*   We want to be clear about what our policy's going to be while
>   we're here in the Void.
> *Janeway:*   You think we should have taken Valen's food.
> *Tuvok:*   Logic suggests we may have to be more opportunistic if we
>   intend to survive.

> *Chakotay:* We may not like Valen's tactics but he and his crew are still alive
> after five years in here.

In response to the conundrum Voyager is seemingly facing in the Void (to be ethical or to survive), Janeway looks for answers in the foundational document of the Federation: "the Federation Charter."

> *Chakotay:* No section on how to exist in a void.
> *Janeway:* No, but I've become convinced that we've got to stick to our principles, not abandon them.
> *Chakotay:* Should the crew be ready to die for those principles?
> *Janeway:* If the alternative means becoming thieves and killers ourselves, yes.

Thus, Janeway reiterates her willingness to die for her (Federation) principles.

However, in a direct rebuke of pragmatic reasoning, Janeway asserts that principled action leads to the optimal outcome. Specifically, she holds that by behaving in a principled manner Voyager can build social capital among the ships trapped in the Void. Through collaboration and solidarity, Janeway argues the ships in the Void can work together to escape. In shaping this reasoning, Janeway draws inspiration from the example of the Federation: "The Federation is based on mutual co-operation. The idea that the whole is greater than the sum of its parts. Voyager can't survive here alone, but if we form a temporary alliance with other ships maybe we can pool our resources and escape." Voyager shares its limited food and medical supplies, as well as joins in common defense, to build trust and establish (what Janeway calls) the "Alliance." Through the Alliance, Voyager's food supplies are enhanced ("One of the crews that joined us had technology that tripled our replicator efficiency...we can feed five hundred people a day now using half the power it took us a few days ago.") Led by Voyager, the Alliance ships escape the Void. Those that refused to become members stay behind.

Villainous Pragmatists

Voyager stands out for the fact that a number of its antagonists are villains (or "bad guys") precisely because they are pragmatists—that is, elide moral principles. This sets *Voyager* apart from other science fiction/fantasy genres, where villains are dastardly not because they lack moral principles (per se) but because of their ultimate goals (e.g., attaining ill-gotten gain [e.g., stealing]; inflicting wanton destruction; seeking revenge; capturing political power, etc.).[143] In the case of *Voyager*, the audience can, broadly speaking, sympathize with its pragmatic antagonists' goals (survival; getting home; arriving at a trade deal; technological advancement), but the villains are *bad guys* precisely because they show little/no scruples is seeking to attain these goals. Four *Voyager* episodes are noteworthy for their villainous pragmatists: "Phage" (1995); "Future's End" (1996); "Think Tank" (1999); and "Equinox" (1999).

"Phage"

As a seeming critique of *neo-pragmatism*, the species known as *Vidiians* is introduced in the episode "Phage". The Vidiians suffer from a condition called the *phage*. The phage destroys the organs of the Vidiians. In response, they steal organs from others to survive. ("We are gathering replacement organs and suitable bio-matter. It is the only way we have to fight the phage.") Thus, the Vidiians have established an *intersubjective agreement* that does not respect/recognize the rights of others to their bodies/organs. ("Our society has been ravaged. Thousands die each day. There is no other way for us to survive.") Janeway is dismayed that the Vidiians would accept the practice of organ theft: "I can't begin to understand what your people have gone through. They may have found a way to ignore the moral implications of what you are doing, but I have no such luxury." Janeway will not take back the organs that were stolen from one of her crew because it would result in the death of their current recipient.

"Future's End"

"Future's End" takes place in the late twentieth century—the year 1996. The action of this episode centers on Henry Starling (played by Ed Begley, Jr.). By the time that Voyager comes into contact with Starling he is a very wealthy technology wizard, like Steve Jobs and Bill Gates. ("Our Mister Starling has built himself quite a corporate empire. Looks like he's got wealth, celebrity and an ego to match.") Starling is only able to introduce "breakthrough" technologies to the twentieth century because years earlier (in 1967) he came upon a space ship from the future. Over time, Starling was able to pilfer technology from the ship.

Voyager's mission in "Future's End" is to discover why a ship from 1996 sought to travel in time, thereby destroying Earth's solar system in the twenty-ninth century. We learn that it will be Starling that will destroy the solar system when he to tries to go to the twenty-ninth century to retrieve more *new* technology for his commercial ventures. He is no longer able to extract usable technology from the ship he found years earlier. ("I've cannibalized the ship itself as much as I can. There's nothing left to base a commercial product on.")

Janeway warns Starling that his attempt to travel into the future will lead to massive catastrophe. Starling, nevertheless, is determined to pursue his goal. Janeway rebukes Starling for his lack of ethics: "You'd destroy an entire city? [Starling threatens to destroy present-day Los Angeles if Janeway tries to stop him.] You don't care about the future, you don't care about the present. Does anything matter to you, Mister Starling?" Starling feels justified in his means and the risk he is creating because his goal is "The betterment of mankind." More specifically, he is driven by technological advancement (at least for his time period):

> My products benefit the entire world. Without me there would be no laptops, no internet, no barcode readers. What's good for Chronowerx [Starling's company] is good for everybody. I can't stop now. One trip to the twenty-ninth century and I can bring back enough technology to start the next ten computer revolutions.
>
> Janeway: In my time, Mister Starling, no human being would dream of endangering the future to gain advantage in the present.

In response, Starling takes an openly pragmatic stance (i.e., centered on the short-term): "Captain, the future you're talking about, that's nine hundred years from now. I can't be concerned about that right now. I have a company to run and a whole world full of people waiting for me to make their lives a little bit better." Voyager destroys Starling and his ship.

"Think Tank"

In "Think Tank" Voyager finds itself being pursued by a species known as the *Hazari*. It is unable to elude them, and Voyager is in serious danger of being destroyed. As they face this peril, an organization that Janeway dubs the *Think Tank* ("a small group of minds") appears, offering Voyager the knowledge necessary to escape the Hazari. But in exchange for this knowledge the Think Tank wants Seven-of-Nine to join their group. We learn that the Think Tank regularly offers knowledge/help in exchange for some prize (normally knowledge).

> We have helped hundreds of clients. We turned the tide in the war between the Bara Plenum and the Motali Empire. Re-ignited the red giants of the Zai Cluster. Just recently, we found a cure for the Vidiian phage . . . Just last month we helped retrieve a Lyridian child's runaway pet. A subspace mesomorph, I might add. We had to invent a whole new scanning technology just to find it.
>
> And what did you ask for as compensation?
>
> One of their transgalactic star charts. The best map of the known galaxy ever created. When we helped the citizens of Rivos Five resist the Borg, all we asked for was the recipe for their famous zoth-nut soup.

Janeway probes the Think Tank's moral/ethical boundaries by asking: "Tell me, is there any job you won't do?" The spokesperson for the group (Kurros—played by Jason Alexander [of "Seinfeld" fame]) explains that "we will not participate in the decimation of an entire species, nor will we design weapons of mass destruction."

Nevertheless, the Think Tank has few scruples in seeking to attain prizes—in this case Seven of Nine. (While human, she is a former member of the Borg collective. Borg modifications have made Seven highly intelligent and capable of telepathic communication.) It was the Think Tank that set the Hazari on Voyager (by placing a bounty on it). In the end, Voyager is able to out-maneuver the Think Tank. But before it is forced to flee, Kurros tells Seven of Nine that she will be dissatisfied living on Voyager, and would have been happier with them—living a life of contemplation and knowledge seeking. ("You know you will never be satisfied here among these people.") Seven-of-Nine, in response, chides the Think Tank for its lack of principles: "Acquiring knowledge is a worthy objective, but its pursuit has obviously not elevated you."

"Equinox"

Arguably the most powerful critique of *pragmatism/neo-pragmatism* (i.e., prioritizing *intersubjective agreement* over actual *justice*) in the Star Trek franchise (and perhaps in all of U.S. television history) is the two-part *Voyager* episode "Equinox". The Equinox is a Federation ship, which like Voyager, was pulled into the Delta Quadrant by the Caretaker. The captain of the Equinox (Rudy Ransom) explains that its isolation and the damage (and loss of life) the ship suffered has eroded the crew's (and his) moral framework:

> When I first realized that we'd be traveling across the Delta quadrant for the rest of our lives I told my crew that we had a duty as Starfleet officers to expand our knowledge and uphold our principles. After a couple of years, we started to forget that we were explorers, and there were times when we nearly forgot that we were human beings.

It turns out that the Equinox killed an intelligent "nucleagenic" life form and harvested it as a power source. (These creatures look like glowing bats.) ("We constructed a containment field that would prevent the life form from vanishing so quickly, but something went wrong.") These life forms contain "high levels of antimatter."

Ransom: We examined the remains and discovered it could be converted to enhance our propulsion systems. It was already dead. What would you have done? We traveled over ten thousand light years in less than two weeks. We'd found our salvation. How could we ignore it?
Janeway: By adhering to the oath you took as Starfleet officers to seek out life, not destroy it.

Ransom defends his actions by pointing to the desperate circumstances that the Equinox found herself:

> It's easy to cling to principles when you're standing on a vessel with its bulkheads intact, manned by a crew that's not starving.

> Janeway rejects this reasoning: It's never easy, but if we turn our backs on our principles, we stop being human. I'm putting an end to your experiments and you are hereby relieved of your command. You and your crew will be confined to quarters.

Ransom and his crew escape from Voyager and resume their journey home. Before they depart they steal Voyager's force "field generator"—thereby seemingly dooming Voyager to destruction by the nucleagenic life forms that are now seeking revenge for the death caused by the Equinox crew.

In part-two of "Equinox," Captain Ransom and his crew continue to do whatever it takes to reach home. They continue to capture and kill the nucleagenic creatures:

> We're going to need more fuel. We've only got enough left to jump another five hundred light years.
>
> Ransom: Fuel. Is that the euphemism we're using now? You mean we need to kill more life forms.
>
> Several more.

Seven-of-Nine was on Equinox as it fled. Ransom tries to entice her to join his crew by arguing that "Janeway clung to her morality at the expense of her crew." Seven-of-Nine refuses and will not give the Equinox vital information. The decision is made to forcibly extract the information, even though doing so will cause Seven-of-Nine permanent and massive brain damage. ("I'm going to extract her cortical array. It contains an index of her memory engrams, but once I've removed it her higher brain functions, language, cognitive skills will be severely damaged.") Janeway is determined to capture Ransom and his crew:

> You're right, I am angry. I'm damned angry. He's a Starfleet Captain, and he's decided to abandon everything this uniform stands for. He's out there right now . . . torturing and murdering innocent life-forms just to get home a little quicker. I'm not going to stand for it. I'm going to hunt him down no matter how long it takes, no matter what the cost. If you want to call that a vendetta, go right ahead.

Voyager captures one of Equinox's crew, and in order to get him to cooperate Janeway comes close to letting the *nucleagenic* creatures kill him. (He relents in time to save himself.)

Captain Janeway communicates with the nucleagenic creatures and enlists their help in stopping Equinox. Janeway explains to the creatures: "We have rules for behavior. The Equinox has broken those rules by killing your species. It's our duty to stop them." The creatures demand: "Give us the Equinox. Give us the Equinox!" ("They insist on destroying the ones who are responsible.") In the face of Commander Tuvok's objection

("We will punish them according to our own rules. They will be impri-
soned. They will lose their freedom"), Janeway agrees to deliver Equinox to
the creatures. In the denouement of "Equinox," Ransom and his ship are
destroyed.

CONCLUSION

Voyager is metaphorically lost in the *developing world*. This allows its creators
to explore motifs and themes different than those dealt with in other iterations of the Star Trek franchise. The strength of *Star Trek: Voyager*—in my
view—as a piece of art/literature is the deep commitment to ethics and
morality that Janeway and her crew display throughout the series. Of course,
this is particularly admirable because losing one's morality/ethics is presumably easy when one is in a very difficult circumstance—like Voyager found
herself. Thus, *Voyager* offers an argument for moral/principled behavior,
and a rejection of *pragmatism*, even in demoralizing and dangerous circumstances. Episodes like "The Void" very powerfully deliver this argument.
Similarly, when confronted with daunting circumstances people may con-
struct *intersubjective agreements* that result in the victimization (death/
murder) of others. Therefore, *Voyager* is particularly critical of an approach
to politics that evades ethics and solely relies on *intersubjective agreement* to
attain stability/success. This critique is especially pointed in the episodes
"Phage," "Future's End," and "Equinox."

CHAPTER 9

Zombies, Star Trek, and International Relations

Abstract The prime optimism of Star Trek, and by implication of humans, is that all able-minded people are capable of speculating about the absolute and the desire to know the absolute is common to the vast majority of us. It is this shared desire that, according to Star Trek, can be basis for human political, social unity. Therefore, the *Borg* and *zombies* are a profound threat to this project of unity and they represent the frightening end of the historic quest to gain absolute knowledge.

Keywords Georg Hegel · The Absolute · Star Trek · Zombies

Daniel W. Drezner, in his book *Theories of International Politics and Zombies*, undertakes the creative task of speculating on the effect on international relations of a global outbreak of zombies.[144] I add to Drezner's innovative approach, by incorporating into it the fictional Borg of the Star Trek franchise. Unlike Drezner's treatment of zombies (where he explicitly eschews using the Marxist paradigm), examining the Star Trek franchise through the lens of international relations theories necessitates the invocation of Marxist arguments concerning global relations and social/political change. Perhaps unsurprisingly, using the *Borg* as a literary device to speculate about international relations leads to a more optimist conclusion than an approach utilizing *zombies*. Moreover, the argument can be made that zombies as a

© The Author(s) 2017
G.A. Gonzalez, *The Absolute and Star Trek*,
DOI 10.1007/978-3-319-47794-7_9

political trope are overtly anti-Marxist (and inherently pessimistic)—insofar as zombies (as ravenous cannibals) could never be incorporated into a global polity.

The optimism in the Borg, when compared to zombies, relates specifically to the issue of speculating about the *absolute*. Both the Borg and zombies are incapable of speculation. As already explained, the prime optimism of Star Trek, and by implication of humans, is that all able minded people are capable of speculating about the absolute and the desire to know the absolute is common to the vast majority of us. It is this shared desire that, according to Star Trek, can be basis for human political, social unity. Therefore, the Borg and zombies are a profound threat to this project of unity and they represent the frightening end of the historic quest to gain *absolute knowledge*. The point is explicitly made that the Borg are unable to *speculate*—as it is noted that the Borg do not create knowledge, but can only appropriate (i.e., "assimilate") it from others.[145] In the end, the Borg are a more optimistic literary device because later we learn (in "I, Borg" 1992—*Next Generation*) that individual Borg (once separated from the collective) are capable of speculation.

ZOMBIES AND BORG

A comparison of zombies and the Borg is apposite. Both are ostensibly mindless, tenacious, and unrelenting. Zombies only seem to growl and mention wanting "brains," and the Borg are similarly single minded and taciturn: "Resistance is futile" is their famous retort to virtually any query. Variations of this theme include "Freedom is irrelevant. Self-determination is irrelevant." Both zombies and the Borg in many ways are beyond reason. Zombies' minimal mental capacity seemingly severely limits their ability to cognate complex ideas. The Borg are highly advanced in technology, but their total commitment to conquering and assimilating others precludes their thoughtful interaction with non-Borg. Upon first encountering the Borg, Captain Picard asks "how do we reason with" them? He is told by someone who has extensive experience in dealing with the Borg that "You don't" ("Q Who" 1989—*Next Generation*). Individual Borg are referred to as intellectually vacuous "drones"[146] and their society is labeled an asocial "hive."[147]

Apart from their evident technological prowess, what makes the Borg such a threat and conundrum for the humans of twenty-fourth century Earth is that the very closed-minded determination of the Borg to "assimilate" all other planets/peoples is a direct challenge to humanity's grand strategy. Earth in the future (according to Star Trek) is predicated on the notion of universal inclusion. Politically, this means that all peoples can be incorporated into a just and fair polity—that is, the *Federation*.

FEDERATION

The *federation* concept of polity in Star Trek is ostensibly predicated on the Marxist ontology of social change and revolution (see Chapter 4). Karl Marx argued that a classless society based on modernity would occur through a series of progressive revolutions. Leon Trotsky, as leader of the Russian Revolution, held that this revolution would inspire other societies to have their own socialist revolution, and, thus, the revolutionary polity would be expanded globally through such examples as set by Russia (and presumably) *et al.*[148]

With humanity basing itself on a *philosophy of self-enhancement* (see Chapter 4), humans come to lead the Federation, and, most importantly, its expansion is predicated on voluntary merger/union. ("The Federation is made up of over a hundred planets *who have allied themselves* for mutual scientific, cultural and defensive benefits" ["Battle Lines" 1993—*Deep Space Nine*]. "The Federation consists of over one hundred and fifty different worlds *who have agreed to share their knowledge and resources in peaceful cooperation*" ["Innocence" 1996—*Voyager*].) Kirk, speaking of the founders of the Federation: "They were humanitarians and statesmen, and they had a dream. A dream that became a reality and spread throughout the stars, a dream that made Mister Spock and me brothers." Indicative of seemingly how the social justice politics (broadly conceived) of the Federation transcends all ethnic, religious (species) divisions, Spock, when asked "do you consider Captain Kirk and yourself brothers?", replied: "Captain Kirk speaks somewhat figuratively and with undue emotion. However, what he says is logical and I do, in fact, agree with it" ("Whom Gods Destroy" 1969—original series).

Voyager episode "The Void" (2001) provides insight into the normative values and political processes that are at the center of *federation*. Voyager is trapped in a "void" in space (where there is no "matter of any kind"). Other ships trapped in the void have taken up the practice of attacking/raiding other trapped ships for supplies as a means of surviving. ("There are more than one hundred fifty ships within scanning range but I'm only detecting life signs on twenty nine of them.")

Through collaboration and solidarity, Janeway argues the ships in the Void can work together to escape. In shaping this reasoning, Janeway draws inspiration from the example of the Federation: "The Federation is based on mutual co-operation. The idea that the whole is greater than the sum of its parts. Voyager can't survive here alone, but if we form a temporary alliance with other ships maybe we can pool our resources and escape." Voyager shares its limited food and medical supplies, as well as joins in common defense, to build trust and establish (what Janeway calls) the "Alliance." Through the Alliance, Voyager's food supplies are enhanced ("One of the crews that joined us had technology that tripled our replicator efficiency...we can feed five hundred people a day now using half the power it took us a few days ago.") Led by Voyager, the Alliance ships escape the Void. Those that refused to become members stay behind.

THE BORG AND FEDERATION FOREIGN POLICY

The Borg, as already alluded to, are not interested in being assimilated (or joining) the Federation as equal partners. The Borg are dead set on forcibly subjugating and incorporating the planets of the Federation into their social structure. Therefore, as initially introduced, the only response the Federation has to deal with the Borg threat is military force.

This is also seemingly true of zombies. This is why Drezner in his analysis of the zombie threat through the lens of different international relations theories concludes that the *realist school* requires virtually no modification in light of the global presence of the undead. Drezner writes: "How would the introduction of flesh-eating ghouls affect world politics? The realist answer is simple if surprising—international relations would be largely unaffected."[149] This is precisely because realist scholars reject *a priori* the Marxist/Trotskyist/Star Trek claim that people can form a single global/interstellar polity.[150] Drezner acknowledges that "realism has a rather dystopic and jaundiced view of the world."[151] He adds that "the failure of humans to cooperate in the presence of reanimated corpses is a common theme that permeates the zombie canon—just as the futility of international cooperation recurs throughout the realist interpretation of history."[152]

Drezner foregoes using the Marxist international relations paradigm[153] to analyze the zombie threat. He suggests (somewhat mockingly) that Marxism has no utility in thinking about humanity's response to zombies since "to Marxists, the undead symbolize the oppressed proletariat."[154] It is untrue, however, that Marxists have nothing to offer in a mind game where zombies are real.[155] To the extent that zombies are the result of an epidemic, Marxists would argue that the result of the plague is the malnutrition; poor water quality; and severely underfunded public health institutions that are the hallmarks of the *underdeveloped* world (and vast pockets of the *developed* world) within capitalism.[156] Therefore, in light of a zombie outbreak, Marxists would respond by arguing that society needs to radically reorient its focus—from one centered on the private accumulation of capital/wealth to one whose prime concern is the prevention of further zombies through worldwide robust/sustained public health programs (broadly conceived).

A parallel can be drawn with the climate change crisis and the capitalist world's response to zombies. In spite of the fact that the global warming phenomenon threatens the very survival of humanity[157] governments around the world (led by the United States[158]) maintain their prime goal of the private creation of wealth—the actual cause of the crisis.[159]

Another way to think about zombies in the international context is that they are a foil to the Marxist idea of internationalism and global solidarity. A sizable zombie population on Earth means that the entirety of the world's population cannot be fully incorporated on the basis of equality into a global polity. Because zombies must ostensibly eat human flesh they cannot live peacefully in a human community. Therefore, the only rational response to zombies is their annihilation. If zombies cannot be completely eradicated, then a permanent state presence is required for the foreseeable future in order to control/manage the undead population. This negates the Marxist contention that the state (i.e., the organized means of violence) will no longer be necessary once communist justice is established worldwide. Henceforth, a sizable zombie population reaffirms the realist stance that states (broadly speaking) are necessary in the modern world, and complete worldwide solidarity is inherently unfeasible (because zombies will forever be outside of the global polity).

As initially presented,[160] the Borg would have the same exact impact on the interstellar system in the world of Star Trek as zombies would have on Earth. The Borg are seemingly incapable or steadfastly unwilling to be incorporated into the Federation, and are determined to, as well as capable of, destroying it. Also, while they do not eat individuals, the Borg do forcibly take individual people and convert (*assimilate*) them into Borg—like infected humans are turned into zombies. In other words, just like zombies, Borg represent a sizable population that cannot be politically incorporated and are a perennially grave and hostile threat that would require an everlasting robust military/state posture—alternatively, the Borg must be completely annihilated.

Indicative of how the Borg represent a shift in political reasoning within the Federation, with the Borg threat Starfleet requires a new surge in military expenditures. When the Borg appears posed to attack the Federation, Starfleet is not prepared, as the weapons being developed to confront the Borg will not be ready any time soon: "I can't believe any of [Starfleet's] new weapons systems can be ready in less than eighteen months." It was worse than that, because Starfleet command is "projecting twenty-four" months before their new weapons would be ready for deployment ("The Best of Both Worlds" 1990—*Next Generation*).

The Federation's desire for survival and its grand strategy of dealing with external threats through appeals to solidarity and inclusion comes into sharp conflict in *The Next Generation* episode "I, Borg" (1992). The Enterprise crew rescues a Borg individual. Picard *et al.* see this Borg as a strategic opportunity. They plan to implant a computer program in the captured Borg that (once he rejoins the collective) would subsequently infect and destroy it. However, as the Enterprise crew nurses the Borg back to health and await for the Borg collective to retrieve the errant drone, the captive Borg comes to see himself not of part of the Borg collective but as an individual. Indicative of this shift, he goes from referring to himself as "third of five" to embracing the name "Hugh." Once Hugh starts to assert himself as a person, not as part of the Borg collective, Picard *et al.* question using him as an instrument of destruction. "I'm having second thoughts about what we're doing here. I mean, programming him like some sort of walking bomb. Sending him back to destroy the others."

More profoundly, once Hugh shows signs of individuality (kindness and compassion), it shows the Enterprise crew that the Borg are not as impervious to appeals for friendship as initially thought. Picard, in a later episode,[161] explains "when Hugh was separated from the Borg collective he began to grow and to evolve into something other than an automaton. He became a person" (i.e., a non-Borg/zombie). Picard calls off the plan to use Hugh to destroy the Borg collective by acknowledging that to do so violates the Federation's normative precepts and modes of operation: "To use him in this manner, we'd be no better than the enemy that we seek to destroy."

Nevertheless, the Borg remain a profound normative challenge for Federation foreign policy. When the Enterprise later encounters the Borg, an admiral asks Picard why he didn't execute the plan to use Hugh to destroy the Borg. Picard responds that "I am … bound by my oath and my conscience to uphold certain principles." The admiral, however, prioritizes the physical safety of the Federation over the ethical precepts it historically has operated upon: "Your priority is to safeguard the lives of Federation citizens, not to wrestle with your conscience. Now I want to make it clear that if you have a similar opportunity in the future, an opportunity to destroy the Borg, you are under orders to take advantage of it."[162]

CONCLUSION

Daniel W. Drezner in his book *Theories of International Politics and Zombies* makes an important contribution to international relations theory. Specifically, he introduces the idea of how to respond to a group of individuals (i.e., zombies) that could never be meaningfully assimilated into peaceful society. In this way, Drezner deftly explores the foundations of key international relations theories. His most important conclusion is that the *realist school* operates on the pessimistic assumption that global unity and solidarity is impossible. Thus, the existence of a sizable zombie population would serve to reinforce/confirm *realist* reasoning about global politics.

One criticism of Drezner's otherwise impressive treatment of the zombie threat is that he does not consider what Marxist international relations theory would hold in response to such a threat. Following from Marxism we can see that arguably the best response to an implacable foe like zombies is political solidarity derived from global social justice. Such a society would presumably have the greatest social capital to cope with (manage) a zombie outbreak. Moreover, a society where all people's biological needs are adequately met would be in the best position to prevent and/or contain a zombie epidemic.

Star Trek, through the literary device of the Borg, offers a similar opportunity to speculate upon international relations theories. Star Trek allows us to see that the Borg (like a zombie) threat would profoundly challenge a polity based on Marxist ideation (the Federation). The Borg (again like zombies) indicates that contrary to Marxist theorizing the known population of sentient beings cannot live in true political harmony. Instead, a sizable portion of humanoids cannot be politically incorporated and necessitate a robust military response.

Nevertheless, Star Trek does take a more optimistic turn when in "I, Borg" a captive Borg responds positively to friendly overtures from the Enterprise crew. It suggests that the Borg collective could be dismantled and the individual Borg could be appealed to through a shared desire to know the *absolute*. This creates the possibility that Borg individuals (unlike with zombies) could be incorporated into the Federation polity. Arguably, the hope that everyone could peacefully live together is the core optimism in Star Trek and presumably in Marxism (i.e., internationalism). Referring to another ostensibly implacable foe (the Romulans):

> *Riker:* A letter to his wife and daughter.
>
> *Data:* Sir, he must have known it would be impossible for us to deliver this.
>
> *Picard:* Today, perhaps. But if there are others with the courage of [Romulan] Admiral Jarok [who defected to prevent war], we may hope to see a day of peace when we can take his letter home.[163]

CHAPTER 10

Conclusion: The Inviability of Analytic Philosophy, as well as Bad and False Infinities

Abstract With analytic philosophers unable to account for the key elements of human existence: consciousness, language, happiness (laughter), etc.—as well as their ignoring of history/time—the *fear of error* need not concern us in contemplating such metaphysical concepts as justice and authenticity. Put differently, analytic philosophers' profound fear of error has not yielded any significant insights into human existence, nor into the existence of humans. Hence, we are free to speculate about the movement of history and how justice as well as authenticity shape that history.

   In this volume I have relied on the broadcast iterations of the Star Trek franchise to speculate about values and practices embedded in the absolute and how embracing these values and practices leads to authentic (fulfilling) lives and a stable thriving society. My argument is that the huge, enduring popularity of Star Trek allows us conclude that this franchise conveys actual knowledge of the *absolute*. In other words, the franchise serves as a guide. This guide tells us to live an authentic/happy life and to achieve a just/sustainable society individuals must be totally committed to social justice, truth, and scientific/intellectual discovery.

   On the one hand, Star Trek effectively lays out how to live an authentic life and how to establish a stable, thriving society. The Star Trek text, on the other hand, also warns us against *bad infinities* and *false infinities*.

Keywords Georg Hegel · Analytic Philosophy · The Absolute · Star Trek

Analytic philosopher Stephen P. Schwartz, in *A Brief History of Analytic Philosophy*, acknowledges that the prime purpose of analytic philosophy is to deny the validity of Hegelian philosophy.[164] Hans-Johann Glock (another analytic philosopher), in his overview of this field, *What is Analytic Philosophy?*, also acknowledges that Hegel is the foil for analytic philosophers, especially his conception of the absolute.[165] Indeed, analytic philosophy would be little more than a sophisticated, exhaustive elaboration of logic if its leading lights were not determinedly united in their commitment to deny/refute the existence of the *absolute*.[166]

Analytic philosophy, however, falters badly when confronted with the human mind.[167] Ostensibly, the two most cogent interpretations of human consciousness from a materialist standpoint are *functionalism* and *identity theory*. Advocates of identity theory hold that the mind is nothing more than biochemical interactions in the brain—in spite of the fact that the biochemical processes of the brain have been thoroughly analyzed and *consciousness* has yet to be located. Functionalism is a theory whereby humans are cast as vessels (computers) that generate outputs in response to inputs (stimuli)—which, if accurate, would reduce free will to nothing more than to a choice of mental states that determine how we respond to stimuli.

Star Trek appropriates the view that human consciousness is a *thing-in-itself* (as argued by Decartes and Hegel) which transcends the organ of the brain. Star Trek uses this notion as an artistic device. In "Turnabout Intruder" (1969—original series), for instance, Kirk (against his will) has his consciousness switched with another person. Data has his body taken over by another person's consciousness ("The Schizoid Man" 1989—*Next Generation*). The *Vulcan Mind Meld* is an artistic device reflecting the notion that the mind is not solely a set of (biochemical) processes nor mental states, but a metaphysical entity.

Schwartz acknowledges that neither identity theory nor functionalism are convincing theories of the human mind. Nevertheless, Schwartz notes (while speaking as a functionalist) that they (as well as all other analytic philosophers) refuse to accept that the human mind cannot be accounted for by materialist explanations: "We are only at the very beginning of the science of mind. No one, at this point, know how, when, or if consciousness . . . can be explained functionally or in some other way consistent with scientific principles."[168] A textbook combination of stubbornness and dogma.

It is noteworthy that comedy/laughter cannot be accounted for by *materialist* conceptions of the human mind. It is a materialist conception that ostensibly prompts Star Trek's creators to write Data (initially) without the capability to partake in humor. With his mind completely consisting of wires, circuits and electrical impulses, Data is in the dark when it comes to jocularity, sarcasm ("The Outrageous Okona" 1988—*Next Generation*).[169]

Materialist conceptions of the mind are of little use when one considers Noam Chomsky's theory of innate language. Chomsky takes note of the fact that children learn languages and concepts with incredible speed. From this, Chomsky reasons that humans have to be born with innate language skills/concepts.[170] Analytic philosophers take this conclusion to support the position that language is a process where we attach words to concepts/pictures in our minds.[171] For this argument to be viable, one must adopt a strong theological position—namely, that some deity (*The Great Programmer*) wrote all concepts into the human mind from the beginning. Pictures/images of all things had to embedded in the brain from the inception of humanity, simply awaiting their invention/creation. Presumably, there are pictures in our minds of future inventions/creations. When finally produced, we will readily recognize them and quickly adopt words to refer to them.

An argument not explicitly rooted in theology, is a theory of language relying on the existence of the absolute. As humans create knowledge this knowledge is accumulated in the *absolute*. Future generations access this knowledge.

Speaking against the idea of the programmed mind, and for its autonomy, is the *Jem'har*—the warrior cast of the *Dominion*. The Jem'har are breed—in other words, they are clones.[172] Nevertheless, they just do not blindly follow the *Founders*—the leaders of the Dominion. The Jemh'dar view the Founders as gods. Maybe genes can be manipulated to make someone more prone to believe in religion, but it is ostensibly impossible to genetically prompt belief in a specified set of religious ideas. (Indicative of this, the Jemh'dar are depicted on occasion as disobeying orders and the chain of command [e.g., "To the Death" 1996—*Deep Space Nine*].) Much more plausible is that the Jemh'dar are indoctrinated (like any other subjugated group) to be subservient to the dominate group—including the state they control. The pertinent point is that to be sentient is by definition to have an autonomous mind—that seemingly has unrestricted access to the *absolute*. Put differently, the mind cannot be genetically (or otherwise) programmed.

While we can reasonably speculate about the relationship between the absolute and sentience as well as learning, knowledge, Star Trek demonstrates that humans are not only social and political animals, but creatures of history as well. What I mean by this is people intuitively refer to history in judging/analyzing their own politics and societies. When a political witch-hunt erupts on the Enterprise, Picard is steeled in his opposition to the hysteria by his knowledge of history:

> Five hundred years ago, military officers would upend a drum on the battle-field sit at it and dispense summary justice. Decisions were quick, punishments severe, appeals denied. Those who came to a drumhead were doomed ("The Drumhead" 1991—*Next Generation*).

More broadly, in *The Next Generation* pilot ("Farpoint Station" 1987) when Q condemns humanity based on its violent history, Picard objects, arguing that humanity is well aware of this history and is determined not to repeat it. (Picard: "That nonsense is centuries behind us!" "Even as far back as . . . we had begun to make rapid progress.") Hence, consistent with a theory that indicates that knowledge of the past is accumulated in the *absolute* that in turn is manifest in children's intellectual prodigiousness, is the fact that humans regularly refer to history to comprehend the present. Thus, human consciousness is figuratively a product of history, and in all likelihood is literally one *vis-à-vis* the absolute.

With analytic philosophers unable to account for the key elements of human existence: consciousness, language, happiness (laughter), etc.—as well as their ignoring of history/time[173]—the *fear of error* need not concern us in contemplating such metaphysic concepts as justice and authenticity. Put differently, analytic philosophers' profound fear of error has not yielded any significant insights into human existence, nor into the existence of humans. Therefore, we are free to speculate about the movement of history and how justice as well as authenticity shape that history (Chapter 3).

In this volume I have relied on the broadcast iterations of the Star Trek franchise to speculate about values and practices embedded in the absolute and how embracing these values and practices leads to authentic (fulfilling) lives and a stable thriving society. My argument is that the huge, enduring popularity of Star Trek allows us conclude that this franchise conveys actual knowledge of the *absolute*. In other words, the franchise serves as a guide. This guide tells us to live an authentic/happy life and to achieve a just/sustainable society individuals must be totally committed to social justice, truth, and scientific/intellectual discovery.

On the one hand, Star Trek effectively lays out how to live an authentic life and how to establish a stable, thriving society. The Star Trek text, on the other hand, also warns us against *bad infinities* and *false infinities*. I take up this matter next.

BAD AND FALSE INFINITIES

As noted in Chapter 1, Hegel wrote of "Bad Infinities," whereas in this volume I have consistently referred to "False Infinities." Hegel's bad infinities relates to social mores, norms at odds with the absolute. Individuals that embrace bad infinities lead unauthentic/unhappy lives. This argument could be made of *pragmatism* and *neo-pragmatism*, where living unprincipled lives results in corruption and misery (Chapter 8). The reason I invoke the phrase false infinities, as opposed to simply bad infinities, is because in the modern era collective/societal bad infinities can lead to societal/global destruction. When Hegel was writing during the late eighteenth and early nineteenth centuries all humans had to worry about was leading unfulfilling/unsatisfactory lives. Today, with weapons of mass destruction and global warming (Chapter 6), we have to be aware that bad infinities can result in false infinities (i.e., the end of civilization). Thus, *Nazism, traditionalism, neoliberalism*, etc. look simply like bad infinities, but in fact they are extremely dangerous (i.e., false infinities) (Chapters 4 and 5). In Chapters 6 and 7, I outline why basing a society on *Dasein* (traditionalism) results in bad infinities—hate, racism, isolated societies. But even worse, the founding of a society on prejudices or the false idea that language is tied to specific Dasein is a straight line to extreme nationalism—that is, Nazism—a false infinity.

The creators of *Voyager* cast Nazism as a traditionalist project. In "The Killing Game" (1998) a German Nazi officer emphasizes the putative greatness of Germany's culture, language (i.e., Dasein) to justify its push for worldwide conquest:

> He's never embraced the Fuhrer or his vision. One does not co-operate with decadent forms of life, one hunts them down and eliminates them. The Kommandant speaks of civilization. The ancient Romans were civilized. The Jews are civilized. But in all its moral decay, Rome fell to the spears of our ancestors as the Jews are falling now. Look at our destiny! The field of red, the purity of German blood. The blazing white circle of the sun that sanctified that blood. No one can deny us, no power on Earth or beyond. Not the Christian Savior, not the God of the Jews. We are driven by the very force that gives life to the universe itself!

The kind of hyper-nationalism (traditionalism) advocated by the likes of the Nazis is extremely dangerous in the modern era. Arguably the worst aspect of a false infinity is that it results in a barbaric "end of history"—that is, the end of speculation and the quest for *Absolute Knowledge* (Chapter 9).

The affirmative argument conveyed in Star Trek is that a stable, sustainable world is only possible through the fruition of the progressive dialectic (Chapter 4), informed by an understanding of the *Absolute* (Chapters 2 and 3). Therefore, to be *authentic* we must commit to the values of *truth, social justice*, and *scientific discovery*. In so doing, we will promote/establish *world government, peace*, and a *sustainable society*. This is the *metaphysics* of Star Trek.

Notes

1. William Maker, ed., *Hegel and Aesthetics* (Albany: State University of New York Press, 2000) (Maker 2000); Kirk Pillow, *Sublime Understanding: Aesthetic Reflection in Kant and Hegel* (Cambridge, MA: MIT Press, 2000) (Pillow 2000); Paul Gordon, *Art as the Absolute: Art's Relation to Metaphysics in Kant, Fichte, Schelling, Hegel, and Schopenhauer* (New York: Bloomsbury Academic, 2015) (Gordon 2015).
2. Donald Phillip Verene, *Hegel's Absolute: An Introduction to Reading the Phenomenology of Spirit* (Albany: State University New York Press, 2007) (Verene 2007); Stephen Houlgate, *Hegel's 'Phenomenology of Spirit': A Reader's Guide* (New York: Bloomsbury Academic, 2013) (Houlgate 2013); Brady Bowman, *Hegel and the Metaphysics of Absolute Negativity* (Cambridge: Cambridge University Press, 2015) (Bowman 2015); James Kreines, *Reason in the World: Hegel's Metaphysics and Its Philosophical Appeal* (New York: Oxford University Press, 2015) (Kreines 2015).
3. Robert L. Perkins, ed., *History and System: Hegel's Philosophy of History* (Albany: State University of New York, 1984) (Perkins 1984); Will Dudley, ed., *Hegel and History* (Albany: State University of New York Press, 2009) (Dudley 2009).
4. Henry Paolucci, "Introduction" in *Hegel: On the Arts*, Henry Paolucci, ed., 2nd ed. (Smyrna, DE: Griffon House, 2001), xix, emphasis added (Paolucci 2001).
5. William Desmond, *Art and the Absolute: A Study of Hegel's Aesthetics* (Albany: State University of New York Press, 1986), xii, emphasis added (Desmond 1986).
6. Lawrence Levine, *Highbrow/Lowbrow: The Emergence of Cultural Hierarchy in America* (Cambridge, MA: Harvard University Press, 1990) (Levine

© The Author(s) 2017
G.A. Gonzalez, *The Absolute and Star Trek,*
DOI 10.1007/978-3-319-47794-7

1990); Jason T. Eberl and Kevin S. Decker, eds. *Star Trek and Philosophy: The Wrath of Kant* (Chicago: Open Court, 1992) (Eberl and Decker 1992).

7. Jack Kaminsky, *Hegel on Art: An Interpretation of Hegel's Aesthetics* (Albany: State University of New York Press, 1962) (Kaminsky 1962).

8. Stephen Mumford, *Metaphysics: A Very Short Introduction* (New York: New York: Oxford University Press, 2012) (Mumford 2012).

9. Jennifer Ann Bates, *Hegel's Theory of Imagination* (Albany: State University of New York Press, 2004) (Bates 2004); Richard Eldridge, *Beyond Representation: Philosophy and Poetic Imagination* (New York: Cambridge University Press, 2011) (Eldridge 2011).

10. Kaminsky, *Hegel on Art*, 29 (Kaminsky 1962).

11. Hans-Johann Glock, *What is Analytic Philosophy?* (New York: Cambridge University Press, 2008), 117–121. (Glock 2008)

12. Ibid., chap. 4.

13. Jan Westerhoff, *Reality: A Very Short Introduction* (New York: Oxford University Press, 2012) (Westerhoff 2012).

14. Siân Ede, *Art and Science* (New York: I. B. Tauris, 2005) (Ede 2005); Martin Kemp, *Seen | Unseen: Art, Science, and Intuition from Leonardo to the Hubble Telescope* (New York: Oxford University Press, 2006) (Kemp 2006); Steven Connor, "Doing without Art," *New Literary History* 42, no. 1 (2011): 53–69 (Connor 2011); Bence Nanay, *Aesthetics as Philosophy of Perception* (New York: Oxford University Press, 2016) (Nanay 2016).

15. E.g., Rebecca Solnit, "Bird by Bird," *New York Times Magazine*, December 7, 2014, MM13 (Solnit 2014); Adam Frank, "Is a Climate Disaster Inevitable?" *New York Times*, January 18, 2015, SR6 (Frank 2015).

16. Kaminsky, *Hegel on Art*, 21 (Kaminsky 1962).

17. George A. Gonzalez, *The Politics of Star Trek: Justice, War, and the Future* (New York: Palgrave Macmillan, 2015) (Gonzalez 2015).

18. In the midst of a labor strike ("Bar Association" 1996—*Deep Space Nine*), a character reads directly from the *Communist Manifesto*: "Workers of the world, unite. You have nothing to lose but your chains." Gareth Stedman Jones, *Karl Marx: Greatness and Illusion* (Cambridge, MA: Harvard University Press, 2016) (Jones 2016).

19. In the 1995 *Deep Space Nine* episode "Past Tense" the phrase "Neo-Trotskists" is used.

20. Reflective of Schmitt's "friend/enemy" reasoning, in *The Next Generation* episode "Face of the Enemy" (1993) the point is made that Romulans have an "absolute certainty about . . . who is a friend and who is an enemy." Also see, Chapter 9 of Gonzalez, *The Politics of Star Trek* (Gonzalez 2015).

21. Peter Singer, *Hegel: A Very Short Introduction* (New York: Oxford University Press, 2001) (Singer 2001a) and *Marx: A Very Short Introduction* (New York: Oxford University Press, 2001) (Singer

2001b); David MacGregor, *Hegel and Marx After the Fall of Communism* (Cardiff: University of Wales Press, [1998] 2014) (MacGregor [1998] 2014) and *The Communist Ideal in Hegel and Marx* (New York: Routledge, 2016) (MacGregor 2016).

22. David Harvey, *Seventeen Contradictions and the End of Capitalism* (New York: Oxford University Press, 2014) (Harvey 2014).

23. Paul Frölich, *Rosa Luxemburg: Her Life and Work* (New York: Howard Fertig, 1969) (Frölich 1969); Stephen Eric Bronner, *Rosa Luxemburg: A Revolutionary for Our Times* (University Park: Pennsylvania State University Press, 1993) (Bronner 1993).

24. Catherine Malabou, *The Future of Hegel: Plasticity, Temporality and Dialectic* (New York: Routledge, 2004) (Malabou 2004).

25. Richard Hanley, *The Metaphysics of Star Trek* (New York: Basic, 1997), xvi, emphasis in original (Hanley 1997).

26. Ibid., xvii.

27. E.g., Rick Worland, "Captain Kirk: Cold Warrior," *Journal of Popular Film & Television* 16, no. 3 (1988): 109–117 (Worland 1988); Mark P. Lagon, "'We Owe It to Them to Interfere:' *Star Trek* and U.S. Statecraft in the 1960s and the 1990s," in *Political Science Fiction*, Donald M. Hassler and Clyde Wilcox, eds. (Columbia: University of South Carolina Press, 1997) (Lagon 1997); Daniel Leonard Bernardi, *Star Trek and History: Race-ing toward a White Future* (New Brunswick, NJ: Rutgers University Press, 1998) (Bernardi 1998); Keith M. Booker, "The Politics of Star Trek," in *The Essential Science Fiction Reader*, J.P. Telotte, ed. (Lexington: University Press of Kentucky, 2008) (Booker 2008).

28. Samuel P. Huntington, *The Clash of Civilizations and the Remaking of World Order* (New York: Simon & Schuster, 1996) (Huntington 1996); Martin Hall and Patrick Thaddeus Jackson, eds., *Civilization Identity* (New York: Palgrave Macmillan, 2007) (Hall and Jackson 2007).

29. Hanley, *The Metaphysics of Star Trek*, 59–64 (Hanley 1997).

30. Ibid., 33.

31. George A. Gonzalez, *The Politics of Star Trek: Justice, War, and the Future* (New York: Palgrave Macmillan, 2015), 39 (Gonzalez 2015).

32. Hans-Johann Glock, *What is Analytic Philosophy?* (New York: Cambridge University Press, 2008) (Glock 2008).

33. Gonzalez, *The Politics of Star Trek*, 115 (Gonzalez 2015).

34. Carlin Romano, *America the Philosophical* (New York: Simon & Schuster, 2012) (Romano 2012); John McCumber, *The Philosophy Scare: The Politics of Reason in the Early Cold War* (Chicago: University of Chicago Press, 2016) (McCumber 2016).

35. Eric Rauchway, *The Great Depression and the New Deal: A Very Short Introduction* (New York: Oxford University Press, 2008) (Rauchway 2008).

36. Robert A. Dahl, and Charles E. Lindblom, "Preface" in *Politics, Economics, and Welfare* (New Haven, CT: Yale University Press, 1976) (Dahl and Lindblom 1976).

37. John McCumber, *Time in a Ditch: American Philosophy in the McCarthy Era* (Evanston, IL: Northwestern University Press, 2001) (McCumber 2001).

38. Gérard Klein, "From the Images of Science to Science Fiction," in *Learning from Other Worlds*, Patrick Parrinder, ed. (Durham, NC: Duke University Press, 2001) (Klein 2001).

39. Alan Shapiro, *Star Trek. Technologies of Disappearance* (Berlin: Avinus Press, 2004) (Shapiro 2004).

40. "Space Seed" (1967; *Star Trek*—original series).

41. "The Borg gain knowledge through assimilation. What they can't assimilate, they can't understand" ("Scorpion" 1997—*Voyager*).

42. Nicholas Wade, "Scientists Seek Ban on Method of Editing the Human Genome," *New York Times*, March 20, 2015, A1 (Wade 2015).

43. Hanley, *The Metaphysics of Star Trek*, 5–10 (Hanley 1997).

44. David S. Stern, ed., *Essays on Hegel's Philosophy of Subjective Spirit* (Albany: State University of New York Press, 2013) (Stern 2013).

45. Darrow Schecter, *The Critique of Instrumental Reason from Weber to Habermas* (New York: Bloomsbury Academic, 2012) (Schecter 2012); Max Horkheimer, *Critique of Instrumental Reason*, trans. Matthew O'Connell (New York: Verso, 2013) (Horkheimer 2013).

46. In the *Critique of Pure Reason*, Kant argues that reason and empiricism can account for all phenomena. Immanuel Kant, *Critique of Pure Reason*, trans. Max Muller (New York: Penguin, 2008 [1781]) (Kant 2008 [1781]).

47. Two observers hold that the religious idea conveyed in the *Voyager* episode "Sacred Ground" (1996) is consonant with New Age beliefs "that spiritual experience are a response to individual spiritual needs and interpretations." Darcee L. McLaren and Jennifer E. Porter, "(Re)Covering Sacred Ground: New Age Spirituality in Star Trek: *Voyager*," in *Star Trek and Sacred Ground: Explorations of Star Trek, Religion, and American Culture*, Jennifer E. Porter and Darcee L. McLaren, eds. (Albany: State University of New York Press, 1999), 108 (McLaren and Porter 1999).

48. When Captain Kirk in *Star Trek Beyond* (2016) is caught lying to Starfleet, he is stripped of his captaincy.

49. Harry G. Frankfurt, *The Reasons of Love* (Princeton: Princeton University Press, 2006) (Frankfurt 2006); Irving Singer, *Philosophy of Love: A Partial Summing-Up* (Cambridge, MA: MIT Press, 2011) (Singer 2011).

50. Naeem Inayatullah, "Bumpy Space: Imperialism and Resistance in *Star Trek: The Next Generation*," in *To Seek Out New Worlds: Science Fiction and World Politics*, Jutta Weldes, ed. (New York: Palgrave Macmillan, 2003) (Inayatullah 2003).

51. Ibid., 55.
52. Ibid., 54.
53. Ibid., 58.
54. Ibid., 55.
55. James M. Demske, *Being, Man, and Death: A Key to Heidegger* (Lexington: University of Kentucky Press, 1970) (Demske 1970).
56. "The Cage" was subsequently broadcast via the episode "The Menagerie" (1966—original series).
57. "City on the Edge of Forever" (1967—original series).
58. Taylor Carman, *Heidegger's Analytic: Interpretation, Discourse and Authenticity in Being and Time* (New York: Cambridge University Press, 2007) (Carman 2007).
59. Sam Polk, a former hedge-fund trader, in a 2014 op-ed piece posited a critical assessment of the ethos that dominates the American finance community: "Wall Street is a toxic culture that encourages the grandiosity of people who are desperately trying to feel powerful." Sam Polk, "For the Love of Money," *New York Times*, January 19, 2014, SR1 (Polk 2014).
60. Karl Marx, *Critique of the Gotha Programme* (London: Electric Book Co., 2001 [1875]), 20 (Marx 2001 [1875]).
61. Karl Marx, *On the Jewish Question*, 1844, http://www.marxists.org/archive/marx/works/1844/jewish-question/. (Marx 1844).
62. Marx, *Critique of the Gotha Programme*, 20 (Marx 2001 [1875]).
63. http://www.st-minutiae.com/academy/literature329/457.txt.
64. Gérard Duménil, and Dominique Lévy, *Capital Resurgent: Roots of the Neoliberal Revolution*, trans. Derek Jeffers (Cambridge, MA: Harvard University Press, 2004) (Duménil and Lévy 2004); Daniel Stedman Jones, *Masters of the Universe: Hayek, Friedman, and the Birth of Neoliberal Politics* (Princeton, N.J.: Princeton University Press, 2012) (Jones 2012).
65. Guin A. McKee, *The Problem of Jobs: Liberalism, Race, and Deindustrialization in Philadelphia* (Chicago: University of Chicago Press, 2009) (McKee 2009); Timothy Williams,"For Shrinking Cities, Destruction Is a Path to Renewal," *New York Times*, November 12, 2013, A15 (Williams 2013).
66. Thomas J. Sugrue, *The Origins of the Urban Crisis: Race and Inequality in Postwar Detroit* (Princeton, NJ: Princeton University Press, 2005) (Sugrue 2005); Joe Drape, "Bankruptcy for Ailing Detroit, but Prosperity for Its Teams," *New York Times*, October 14, 2013, A1 (Drape 2013); Rebecca J. Kinney, *Beautiful Wasteland: The Rise of Detroit as America's Postindustrial Frontier* (Minneapolis: University of Minnesota Press, 2016) (Kinney 2016).
67. Carol Poh Miller and Robert Wheeler, *Cleveland: A Concise History* (Bloomington: Indiana University Press, 2009) (Miller and Wheeler 2009).

68. Mary Elizabeth Gallagher, *Contagious Capitalism: Globalization and the Politics of Labor in China* (Princeton: Princeton University Press, 2005) (Gallagher 2005); Kelly Sims Gallagher, *China Shifts Gears: Automakers, Oil, Pollution, and Development* (Cambridge, MA: MIT Press, 2006) (Gallagher 2006); Louis Uchitelle, "Goodbye, Production (and Maybe Innovation)," *New York Times*, December 24, 2006, sec. 3 p. 4; (Uchitelle 2006); Peter S. Goodman, "U.S. and Global Economies Slipping in Unison," *New York Times*, August 24, 2008, A1 (Goodman 2008); David Koistinen, *Confronting Decline: The Political Economy of Deindustrialization in Twentieth-Century New England* (Gainesville: University Press of Florida, 2013) (Koistinen 2013).

69. Susan M. Wachter, and Kimberly A. Zeuli, eds., *Revitalizing American Cities* (Philadelphia: University of Pennsylvania Press, 2013) (Wachter and Zeuli 2013); Monica Davey, "A Picture of Detroit Ruin, Street by Forlorn Street," *New York Times*, February. 18, 2014, A1 (Davey 2014); Jon Hurdle, "Philadelphia Forges Plan To Rebuild From Decay," *New York Times*, January 1, 2014, B1 (Hurdle 2014).

70. Deborah K. Padgett, Benjamin F. Henwood, Sam J. Tsemberis. *Housing First: Ending Homelessness, Transforming Systems, and Changing Lives* (New York: Oxford University Press, 2015) (Padgett, Henwood, and Tsemberis 2015); Craig Willse, *The Value of Homelessness: Managing Surplus Life in the United States* (Minneapolis: University of Minnesota Press, 2015) (Willse 2015).

71. Kristin S. Seefedt and John D. Graham, *America's Poor and the Great Recession* (Bloomington: Indiana University Press, 2013) (Seefedt and Graham 2013); "Ten States Still Have Fewer Jobs Since Recession," Reuters, March 25, 2016 ("Ten States Still" 2016).

72. Erik Brynjolfsson, and Andrew McAfee, *Race Against the Machine: How the Digital Revolution is Accelerating Innovation, Driving Productivity, and Irreversibly Transforming Employment and the Economy* (San Francisco: Digital Frontier Press, 2012) (Brynjolfsson and McAfee 2012); Cecilia Kang, "New Robots in the Workplace: Job Creators or Job Terminators?" *Washington Post*, March 6, 2013. Web (Kang 2013); Claire Cain Miller, "Smarter Robots Move Deeper Into Workplace," *New York Times*, December 16, 2014, A1 (Miller 2014); Farhad Manjoo, "Uber's Business Model Could Change Your Work," *New York Times*, January 29, 2015, B1 (Manjoo 2015); Zeynep Tufekci, "The Machines Are Coming," *New York Times*, April 19, 2015, SR4 (Tufekci 2015).

73. Paul Krugman, "Robots and Robber Barons," *New York Times*, December 10, 2012, A27 (Krugman 2012).

74. Paul Frölich, *Rosa Luxemburg: Her Life and Work* (New York: Howard Fertig, 1969) (Frölich 1969); Stephen Eric Bronner, *Rosa Luxemburg: A*

Revolutionary for Our Times (University Park: Pennsylvania State University Press, 1993) (Bronner 1993).

75. James M. McPherson, *Abraham Lincoln and the Second American Revolution* (New York: Oxford University Press, 1992) (McPherson 1992); James Oakes, *Freedom National: The Destruction of Slavery in the United States* (New York: W.W. Norton & Company, 2012) (Oakes 2012).

76. Sidney Hook, *Towards the Understanding of Karl Marx* (New York: John Day, 1933), 294–295 (Hook 1933).

77. James P. Cannon, *The History of American Trotskyism: Report of a Participant* (New York: Pioneer Publishers, 1944) (Cannon 1944); Constance Ashton Myers, *The Prophet's Army: Trotskyists in America, 1928–1941* (Westport, CT: Greenwood Press, 1977) (Myers 1977); A. Belden Fields, *Trotskyism and Maoism: Theory and Practice in France and the United States* (New York: Praeger, 1988), chap. 4 (Fields 1988); Bryan D. Palmer, *James P. Cannon and the Origins of the American Revolutionary Left, 1890–1928* (Urbana: University of Illinois Press, 2010) (Palmer 2010).

78. In the midst of a labor strike ("Bar Association" 1996—*Deep Space Nine*), a character reads directly from the *Communist Manifesto*: "Workers of the world, unite. You have nothing to lose but your chains."

79. Catherine Malabou, *The Future of Hegel: Plasticity, Temporality and Dialectic* (New York: Routledge, 2004) (Malabou 2004).

80. Michael Inwood, *Heidegger: A Very Short Introduction* (New York: Oxford University Press, 2000) (Inwood 2000).

81. Joseph W. Bendersky, *Carl Schmitt: Theorist for the Reich* (Princeton, NJ: Princeton University Press, 1983) (Bendersky 1983).

82. Shadia B. Drury, *Leo Strauss and the American Right* (New York: St. Martin's Press, 1997) (Drury 1997); Michael P. Zuckert and Catherine H. Zuckert, *Leo Strauss and the Problem of Political Philosophy* (Chicago: University of Chicago Press, 2014) (Zuckert and Zuckert 2014).

83. Michael Cowan, *Cult of the Will: Nervousness and German Modernity* (University Park, PA: Penn State University Press, 2013) (Cowan 2013).

84. This is the title of a Nazi propaganda film, trumpeting the putative unity of the German people behind the Hitler regime.

85. Jane Caplan, *Nazi Germany (Short Oxford History of Germany)* (New York: Oxford University Press, 2008) (Caplan 2008); Ian Kershaw, *Hitler, the Germans, and the Final Solution* (New Haven, CT: Yale University Press, 2009) (Kershaw 2009), and *Hitler: A Biography* (New York: Norton, 2010) (Kershaw 2010).

86. Friedrich Nietzsche, *Beyond Good & Evil: Prelude to a Philosophy of the Future* (New York: Vintage, 1989 [1886]) (Nietzsche 1989 [1886]).

87. James M. Demske, *Being, Man, and Death: A Key to Heidegger* (Lexington: University of Kentucky Press, 1970) (Demske 1970).

88. Bendersky, *Carl Schmitt* (Bendersky 1983).

89. "The specific political distinction to which political actions and motives can be reduced is that between friend and enemy." Carl Schmitt, *The Concept of the Political*, expanded edition (Chicago: University of Chicago University, 2007 [1929]), 26 (Schmitt 2007 [1929]).

90. Drury, *Leo Strauss and the American Right*, 23 (Drury 1997).

91. Caplan, *Nazi Germany* (Caplan 2008); Jeffrey Herf, *The Jewish Enemy: Nazi Propaganda during World War II and the Holocaust* (Cambridge, MA: Harvard University Press, 2008) (Herf 2008).

92. The script notes to the movie: "A Third World War. Nuclear explosions, environmental disasters, tens of millions dead. The United States ceases to exist. All political authority vanishes. Humanity teetering on the edge of the Second Dark Age." http://www.st-minutiae.com/academy/litera ture329/fc.txt.

93. Schmitt, *The Concept of the Political*, 27 (Schmitt 2007 [1929]).

94. Peter Singer, *Marx: A Very Short Introduction* (New York: Oxford University Press, 2001) (Singer 2001b).

95. The following is in the 1995 movie script:
Scrimm (2063 resident of Earth): "Where are you from most recently?"
Picard: "California. San Francisco"
Scrimm: "Beautiful city. Used to be, anyway. I didn't think anyone still lived there." http://www.st-minutiae.com/academy/literature329/fc.txt.

96. "The Shipment" (2003—*Enterprise*).

97. Zuckert and Zuckert, *Leo Strauss and the Problem of Political Philosophy* (Zuckert and Zuckert 2014).

98. Anne Mackenzie Pearson, "From Thwarted Gods to Reclaimed Mystery?: An Overview of the Depiction of Religion in *Star Trek*," in *Star Trek and Sacred Ground: Explorations of Star Trek, Religion, and American Culture*, Jennifer E. Porter and Darcee L. McLaren, eds. (Albany: State University of New York Press, 1999) (Pearson 1999).

99. John H. McWhorter points out that humans (regardless of language) see the world (i.e., *reality*) in the same way. *The Language Hoax: Why the World Looks the Same in Any Language* (New York: Oxford University Press, 2014) (McWhorter 2014).

100. Martin Heidegger, *Being and Time* (New York: Harper Perennial Modern Classics, 2008 [1927]) (Heidegger 2008 [1927]).

101. Jennifer Anna Gosetti-Ferencei, *Heidegger, Holderlin, and the Subject of Poetic Language: Toward a New Poetics of Dasein* (New York: Forham University Press, 2009) (Gosetti-Ferencei 2009); John Haugeland, *Dasein Disclosed: John Haugeland's Heidegger*, Joseph Rouse, ed. (Cambridge, MA: Harvard University Press, 2013) (Haugeland 2013).

102. K. David Harrison, *When Languages Die: The Extinction of the World's Languages and the Erosion of Human Knowledge* (New York: Oxford University Press, 2008) (Harrison 2008).

103. John McCumber, *The Company of Words: Hegel, Language, and Systematic Philosophy* (Chicago: Northwestern University, 1993) (McCumber 1993); Jere O'Neill Surber, ed., *Hegel and Language* (Albany: State University of New York Press, 2006) (O'Neill 2006); Jim Vernon, *Hegel's Philosophy of Language* (London: Continuum, 2007) (Vernon 2007).

104. Karin Blair, *Meaning in Star Trek* (New York: Warner, 1977) (Blair 1977) and "The Garden in the Machine: The Why of Star Trek," *Journal of Popular Culture* 13, no. 2 (fall 1979): 310–319 (Blair 1979); Ina Rae Hark, "Star Trek and Television's Moral Universe," *Extrapolation* 20, no. 1 (spring 1979): 20–37 (Hark 1979); Taylor Harrison, *et al.*, eds. *Enterprise Zones: Critical Positions on Star Trek* (Boulder, CO: Westview, 1996) (Harrison, *et al.* 1996); Thomas Richards, *The Meaning of Star Trek* (New York: Doubleday, 1997) (Richards 1997); Daniel Leonard Bernardi, *Star Trek and History: Race-ing Toward a White Future* (Newark, NJ: Rutgers University Press, 1998) (Bernardi 1998); Jon Wagner and Jan Lundeen, *Deep Space and Sacred Time: Star Trek in the American Mythos* (Westport, CT: Praeger, 1998) (Wagner and Lundeen 1998); Robin Roberts, *Sexual Generations: "Star Trek: The Next Generation" and Gender* (Chicago: University of Illinois Press, 1999) (Roberts 1999); Alan N. Sharpio, *Star Trek: Technologies of Disappearance* (Berlin: AVINUS Verlag, 2004); David Greven, *Gender and Sexuality in Star Trek: Allegories of Desire in the Television Series and Films* (Jefferson, NC: MacFarland, 2009) (Greven 2009).

105. During "Attached" (1993—*Next Generation*) it is noted that Earth's world government was formed in 2150.

106. "Attached" (1993—*Next Generation*).

107. V.I. Lenin, *Imperialism: The Highest Stage of Capitalism* (New York: Pluto, 1996 [1917]) (Lenin 1996 [1917]).

108. Christopher Read, *Lenin: A Revolutionary Life* (New York: Routledge, 2005) (Read 2005).

109. Daryl Johnson, and Mark Potok, *Right-Wing Resurgence: How a Domestic Terrorist Threat is Being Ignored* (Lanham, MD: Rowman & Littlefield, 2012) (Johnson and Potok 2012); Joseph E. Uscinski and Joseph M. Parent, *American Conspiracy Theories* (New York: Oxford University Press, 2014) (Uscinski and Parent 2014); Neil MacFarquhar, "Russia, Jailer of Local Separatists, Hosts Foreign Ones," *New York Times*, September 26, 2016, A6 (MacFarquhar 2016); Liam Stack, "Globalism: A Far-Right Conspiracy Theory Buoyed by Trump," *New York Times*, November 14, 2016. Web (Stack 2016).

110. Mark Mozower, *Governing the World: The History of an Idea* (New York: Penguin Press, 2012), 26–30 (Mozower 2012).

111. Mark Maslin, *Global Warming: A Very Short Introduction* (New York: Oxford University Press, 2009) (Maslin 2009); James Lawrence Powell, *The Inquisition of Climate Science* (New York: Columbia University Press, 2011) (Powell 2011); George A. Gonzalez, *American Empire and the Canadian Oil Sands* (New York: Palgrave MacMillan, 2016) (Gonzalez 2016a).

112. Justin Gillis, "Ending Its Summer Melt, Arctic Sea Ice Sets a New Low That Leads to Warnings," *New York Times*, September 20, 2012, A8 (Gillis 2012).

113. John M. Broder, "Climate Talks Yield Commitment to Ambitious, but Unclear, Actions," *New York Times*, December 9, 2012, A13 (Broder 2012).

114. Justin Gillis, and John M. Broder, "With Carbon Dioxide Emissions at Record High, Worries on How to Slow Warming," *New York Times*, December 3, 2012, A6 (Gillis and Broder 2012).

115. Kurkpatrick Dorsey, *Whales and Nations: Environmental Diplomacy on the High Seas* (Seattle: University of Washington Press, 2013) (Dorsey 2013).

116. John Firor, and Judith Jacobsen, *The Crowded Greenhouse: Population, Climate Change, and Creating a Sustainable World* (New Haven, CT: Yale University Press, 2002) (Firor and Jacobsen 2002).

117. Walter K. Dodds, *Humanity's Footprint: Momentum, Impact, and Our Global Environment* (New York: Columbia University Press, 2008) (Dodds 2008); Thomas Robertson, *The Malthusian Moment: Global Population Growth and the Birth of American Environmentalism* (New Brunswick, NJ: Rutgers University Press, 2012) (Robertson 2012).

118. Matthew Connelly, *Fatal Misconception: The Struggle to Control World Population* (Cambridge, MA: Harvard University Press, 2008) (Connelly 2008).

119. Michael Egan, *Barry Commoner and the Science of Survival: The Remaking of American Environmentalism* (Cambridge, MA: MIT Press, 2009) (Egan 2009); Paul Sabin, *The Bet: Paul Ehrlich, Julian, and Our Gamble over Earth's Future* (New Haven, CT: Yale University Press, 2013) (Sabin 2013).

120. Eric D. Smith, *Globalization, Utopia, and Postcolonial Science Fiction* (New York: Palgrave Macmillan, 2012) (Smith 2012).

121. Arthur M. Schlesinger, *The Disuniting of America: Reflections on a Multicultural Society* (New York: W.W. Norton, 1988) (Schlesinger 1988); Derek Rubin, and Jaap Verheul, eds., *American Multiculturalism after 9/11: Transatlantic Perspectives* (Amsterdam: Amsterdam University Press, 2010) (Rubin and Verheul 2010); Denis Lacorne, *Religion in America: A Political History* (New York: Columbia University Press,

2001) (Lacorne 2001); Alexis de Tocqueville, *Democracy in America*, trans. by Harvey C. Mansfield and Delba Winthrop (Chicago: University of Chicago Press, 2011 [1835]) (De Tocqueville 2011 [1835]).

122. *Star Trek: Nemesis* (2002).

123. "Transfigurations" (1990—*Next Generation*).

124. Harlow Giles Unger, *Lafayette* (Hoboken, NJ: Wiley, 2003) (Unger 2003); Craig Nelson, *Thomas Paine: Enlightenment, Revolution, and the Birth of Modern Nations* (New York: Penguin, 2007) (Nelson 2007); Joseph F. Kett, *Merit: The History of a Founding Ideal From the American Revolution to the Twenty-First Century* (Ithaca, NY: Cornell University Press, 2013) (Kett 2013).

125. James M. McPherson, *Battle Cry of Freedom: The Civil War Era* (New York: Oxford University Press, 2003) (McPherson 2003).

126. Karl Marx, *Critique of the Gotha Programme* (London: Electric Book Co., 2001 [1875]), 20 (Marx 2001 [1875]).

127. McWhorter, *The Language Hoax* (McWhorter 2014).

128. Samuel P. Huntington, *The Clash of Civilizations and the Remaking of World Order* (New York: Simon & Schuster, 1996) (Huntington 1996); David Brooks, "Saving the System," *New York Times*, April 29, 2014, A23 (Brooks 2014).

129. Adam Adatto Sandel, *The Place of Prejudice: A Case for Reasoning in the World* (Cambridge, MA: Harvard University Press, 2014), 8 (Sandel 2014).

130. Ibid., 6.

131. Martin Heidegger, *Being and Time* (New York: Harper Perennial Modern Classics, 2008 [1927]) (Heidegger 2008 [1927]).

132. This is also true of Vulcans-humans and Romulans-humans.

133. For a full list of Klingon rituals see: http://www.klingon.org/database/rituals.html#anchor714236.

134. Piotr Hoffman, "Death, Time, History: Division II of *Being and Time*," in *The Cambridge Companion to Heidegger*, Charles B. Guigon, ed. (New York: Cambridge University Press, 2006), 239 (Hoffman 2006).

135. Robert Danisch, *Pragmatism, Democracy, and the Necessity of Rhetoric* (Columbia: University of South Carolina Press, 2007) (Danisch 2007); Larry A. Hickman, *Pragmatism as Post-Modernism: Lessons from John Dewey* (New York: Forham University Press, 2007) (Hickman 2007); Alan Malachowski, *The New Pragmatism* (Montreal: McGill-Queen's University Press, 2010) (Malachowski 2010); Michael Bacon, *Pragmatism* (Cambridge: Polity, 2012) (Bacon 2012).

136. Daniel Berthold-Bond, *Hegel's Grand Synthesis: A Study of Being, Thought, and History* (Albany: State University of New York Press, 1989) (Berthold-Bond 1989).

137. Louis Menand, *The Metaphysical Club* (New York: Farrar, Straus, and Giroux, 2001), xii (Menand 2001).

138. Richard Rorty, *Philosophy and the Mirror of Nature* (Princeton: Princeton University Press, 1981) (Rorty 1981); Michael Bacon, *Richard Rorty: Pragmatism and Political Liberalism* (Lanham: Lexington Books, 2007) (Bacon 2007); Neil Gross, *Richard Rorty: The Making of an American Philosopher* (Chicago: University of Chicago Press, 2008) (Gross 2008).
139. "Crossover" (1994—*Deep Space Nine*).
140. John F. Burns, "U.N. Panel To Assess Drone Use," *New York Times*, January 25, 2013, A4 (Burns 2013); Lloyd C. Gardner, *Killing Machine: The American Presidency in the Age of Drone Warfare* (New York: New Press, 2013) (Gardner 2013); Thom Shanker, "Simple, Low-Cost Drones a Boost for U.S. Military," *New York Times*, January 25, 2013, A12 (Shanker 2013); Declan Walsh, and Ihsanullah Tipu Mehsud, "Civilian Deaths in Drone Strikes Cited in Report," *New York Times*, October 22, 2013, A1 (Walsh and Mehsud 2013).
141. George A. Gonzalez, *The Politics of Star Trek: Justice, War, and the Future* (New York: Palgrave MacMillan, 2015), chap. 10 (Gonzalez 2015).
142. Michael Walzer, *Thinking Politically: Essays in Political Theory*, David Miller, ed. (New Haven: Yale University Press, 2007), chap. 1 (Walzer 2007).
143. Daniel H. Nexon and Iver B. Neuman, *Harry Potter and International Relations* (Lanham, MD: Rowman & Littlefield, 2006) (Nexon and Neuman 2006); Jason Dittmer, *Captain America and the Nationalist Superhero* (Philadelphia: Temple University Press, 2012) (Dittmer 2012); George A. Gonzalez, "*Justice League Unlimited* and the Politics of Globalization," *Foundation: The International Review of Science Fiction* 45, no. 123 (2016): 5-13 (Gonzalez 2016b).
144. Daniel W. Drezner, *Theories of International Politics and Zombies*, revised edn. (Princeton: Princeton University Press, 2015) (Drezner 2015).
145. "The Borg gain knowledge through assimilation. What they can't assimilate, they can't understand" ("Scorpion" 1997—*Voyager*).
146. "Scorpion" (1997—*Voyager*).
147. "I, Borg" (1992—*Next Generation*).
148. Issac Deutscher, *The Prophet Armed: Trotsky 1879–1921*, vol. 1 (New York: Oxford University Press, 1963) (Deutscher 1963); Leon Trotsky, *History of the Russian Revolution* (New York: Pathfinder, 1980 [1933]) (Trotsky 1980 [1933]).
149. Drezner, *Theories of International Politics and Zombies*, 40 (Drezner 2015).
150. Mark Mozower, *Governing the World: The History of an Idea* (New York: Penguin Press, 2012) (Mozower 2012).
151. Drezner, *Theories of International Politics and Zombies*, 38 (Drezner 2015).
152. Ibid., 39.
153. Vendulka Kubálková, and Albert A. Cruickshank, *Marxism and International Relations* (New York: Oxford University Press, 1989)

(Kubálková and Cruickshank 1989); Neil Smith, *Uneven Development: Nature, Capital, and the Production of Space*, 3rd ed. (Athens: University of Georgia Press, 2008) (Smith 2008).

154. Drezner, *Theories of International Politics and Zombies*, 16 (Drezner 2015). Marxists view zombies in popular culture as an attempt to scare people into supporting the capitalist status quo from the mayhem and mortal threat they conjure. Roland Vegso, *The Naked Communist: Cold War Modernism and the Politics of Popular Culture* (New York: Fordham University Press, 2013) (Vegso 2013).

155. Chris Harman, *Zombie Capitalism: Global Crisis and the Relevance of Marx* (Chicago: Haymarket Books, 2010) (Harman 2010).

156. Max Brooks, *World War Z: An Oral History of the Zombie War* (New York: Three Rivers Press, 2007) (Brooks 2007); Henry A. Giroux, *Zombie Politics and Culture in the Age of Casino Capitalism* (New York: Peter Lang, 2010) (Giroux 2010).

157. Elizabeth Kolbert, *The Sixth Extinction: An Unnatural History* (New York: Henry Holt, 2014) (Kolbert 2014).

158. Michael H. Hunt, *The American Ascendancy: How the United States Gained and Wielded Global Dominance* (Chapel Hill: University of North Carolina Press, 2007) (Hunt 2007); Joan Hoff, *A Faustian Foreign Policy: From Woodrow Wilson to George W. Bush* (New York: Cambridge University Press, 2008) (Hoff 2008); George A. Gonzalez, *Energy and the Politics of the North Atlantic* (Albany: State University of New York Press, 2013) (Gonzalez 2013) and *American Empire and the Canadian Oil Sands* (New York: Palgrave MacMillan, 2016) (Gonzalez 2016a).

159. Gérard Duménil and Dominique Lévy, *Capital Resurgent: Roots of the Neoliberal Revolution*, trans. Derek Jeffers (Cambridge: Harvard University Press, 2004) (Duménil and Lévy 2004); Daniel Stedman Jones, *Masters of the Universe: Hayek, Friedman, and the Birth of Neoliberal Politics* (Princeton, N.J.: Princeton University Press, 2012) (Jones 2012); Adrian Parr, *The Wrath of Capital: Neoliberalism and Climate Change Politics* (New York: Columbia University Press, 2013) (Parr 2013).

160. "Q Who" (1989—*Next Generation*) and "Best of Both Worlds" (1990—*Next Generation*).

161. "Descent" (1993—*Next Generation*).

162. Ibid.

163. "Defector" (1990—*Next Generation*).

164. Stephen P. Schwartz, *A Brief History of Analytic Philosophy: From Russell to Rawls* (West Sussex, UK: Wiley-Blackwell, 2012), 27–29, 38 (Schwartz 2012).

165. Hans-Johann Glock, *What is Analytic Philosophy?* (New York: Cambridge University Press, 2008), 30–34 (Glock 2008).

166. Nicholas Capaldi, *The Enlightenment Project in the Analytic Conversation* (Boston: Kluwer Academic Publishers, 1998) (Capaldi 1998).

167. Josh Weisberg, *Consciousness* (Cambridge, MA: Polity, 2014) (Weisberg 2014).

168. Schwartz, *A Brief History of Analytic Philosophy*, 192 (Schwartz 2012).

169. Perhaps because a materialist conception of the mind is unrealistic, artistically uninteresting, or both, later, we learn that Data's android "brother," Lore, does have emotions ("Datalore" 1988—*Next Generation*), and Data ultimately comes to have emotions through an "emotion chip" ("Brothers" 1990—*Next Generation*; *Star Trek: Generations* 1994). I note in Chapters 2 and 3 that the Data character was always written with emotions—at a minimum desire and loyalty.

170. James McGilvray, *Chomsky: Language, Mind, and Politics* (Cambridge: Polity, 1999) (McGilvray 1999); Noam Chomsky, *Language and Mind*, 3rd ed. (New York: Cambridge University Press, 2006) (Chomsky 2006).

171. Schwartz, *A Brief History of Analytic Philosophy*, 182 (Schwartz 2012).

172. Stephen E. Levick, *Clone Being: Exploring the Psychological and Social Dimensions* (Lanham, MD: Rowman & Littlefield, 2003) (Levick 2003); Arlene Judith Klotzko, *A Clone of Your Own?* (New York: Cambridge University Press, 2006) (Klotzko 2006).

173. Peter Osborne, *The Politics of Time: Modernity and Avant-Garde* (New York: Verso, 1995) (Osborne 1995); John McCumber, *Time and Philosophy: A History of Continental Thought* (Montreal: McGill-Queen's University Press, 2011) (McCumber 2011).

BIBLIOGRAPHY

Bacon, Michael. *Richard Rorty: Pragmatism and Political Liberalism*. Lanham: Lexington Books, 2007.

Bacon, Michael. *Pragmatism*. Cambridge: Polity, 2012.

Bates, Jennifer Ann. *Hegel's Theory of Imagination*. Albany: State University of New York Press, 2004.

Bendersky, Joseph W. *Carl Schmitt: Theorist for the Reich*. Princeton: Princeton University Press, 1983.

Bernardi, Daniel Leonard. *Star Trek and History: Race-ing toward a White Future*. New Brunswick: Rutgers University Press, 1998.

Berthold-Bond, Daniel. *Hegel's Grand Synthesis: A Study of Being, Thought, and History*. Albany: State University of New York Press, 1989.

Blair, Karin. *Meaning in Star Trek*. New York: Warner, 1977.

Blair, Karin. "The Garden in the Machine: The Why of Star Trek." *Journal of Popular Culture* 13, no. 2 (fall 1979): 310–319.

Booker, Keith M. "The Politics of Star Trek." In *The Essential Science Fiction Reader*, ed. J.P. Telotte. Lexington: University Press of Kentucky, 2008.

Bowman, Brady. *Hegel and the Metaphysics of Absolute Negativity*. Cambridge: Cambridge University Press, 2015.

Broder, John M. "Climate Talks Yield Commitment to Ambitious, but Unclear, Actions," *New York Times*, December 9, 2012, A13.

Bronner, Stephen Eric. *Rosa Luxemburg: A Revolutionary for Our Times*. University Park: Pennsylvania State University Press, 1993.

Brooks, David. "Saving the System." *New York Times*, April 29, 2014, A23.

© The Author(s) 2017
G.A. Gonzalez, *The Absolute and Star Trek*,
DOI 10.1007/978-3-319-47794-7

Brooks, Max. *World War Z: An Oral History of the Zombie War.* New York: Three Rivers Press, 2007.

Brynjolfsson, Erik, and Andrew McAfee. *Race Against the Machine: How the Digital Revolution is Accelerating Innovation, Driving Productivity, and Irreversibly Transforming Employment and the Economy.* San Francisco: Digital Frontier Press, 2012.

Burns, John F. "U.N. Panel To Assess Drone Use," *New York Times,* January 25, 2013, A4.

Cannon, James P. *The History of American Trotskyism: Report of a Participant.* New York: Pioneer Publishers, 1944).

Capaldi, Nicholas. *The Enlightenment Project in the Analytic Conversation.* Boston: Kluwer Academic Publishers, 1998.

Caplan, Jane. *Nazi Germany (Short Oxford History of Germany).* New York: Oxford University Press, 2008.

Carman, Taylor. *Heidegger's Analytic: Interpretation, Discourse and Authenticity in Being and Time.* New York: Cambridge University Press, 2007.

Chomsky, Noam. *Language and Mind* (3rd edn.). New York: Cambridge University Press, 2006.

Connelly, Matthew. *Fatal Misconception: The Struggle to Control World Population.* Cambridge, MA: Harvard University Press, 2008.

Connor, Steven. "Doing without Art." *New Literary History* 42, no. 1 (2011): 53–69.

Cowan, Michael. *Cult of the Will: Nervousness and German Modernity.* University Park, PA: Penn State University Press, 2013.

Dahl, Robert A., and Charles E. Lindblom. "Preface." In *Politics, Economics, and Welfare.* New Haven: Yale University Press, 1976.

Danisch, Robert. *Pragmatism, Democracy, and the Necessity of Rhetoric.* Columbia: University of South Carolina Press, 2007.

Davey, Monica. "A Picture of Detroit Ruin, Street by Forlorn Street," *New York Times,* February 18, 2014, A1.

De Tocqueville, Alexis. *Democracy in America* (trans: Harvey C. Mansfield and Delba Winthrop). Chicago: University of Chicago Press, 2011 [1835].

Demske, James M. *Being, Man, and Death: A Key to Heidegger.* Lexington: University of Kentucky Press, 1970.

Desmond, William. *Art and the Absolute: A Study of Hegel's Aesthetics.* Albany: State University of New York Press, 1986.

Deutscher, Issac. *The Prophet Armed: Trotsky 1879–1921* (Vol. 1). New York: Oxford University Press, 1963.

Dittmer, Jason. *Captain America and the Nationalist Superhero.* Philadelphia: Temple University Press, 2012.

Dodds, Walter K. *Humanity's Footprint: Momentum, Impact, and Our Global Environment.* New York: Columbia University Press, 2008.

Dorsey, Kurkpatrick. *Whales and Nations: Environmental Diplomacy on the High Seas*. Seattle: University of Washington Press, 2013.

Drape, Joe. "Bankruptcy for Ailing Detroit, but Prosperity for Its Teams," *New York Times*, October 14, 2013, A1.

Drezner, Daniel W. *Theories of International Politics and Zombies* (revised edn.). Princeton: Princeton University Press, 2015.

Drury, Shadia B. *Leo Strauss and the American Right*. New York: St. Martin's Press, 1997.

Dudley, Will, ed. *Hegel and History*. Albany: State University of New York Press, 2009.

Duménil, Gérard, and Dominique Lévy. *Capital Resurgent: Roots of the Neoliberal Revolution* (trans: Derek Jeffers). Cambridge, MA: Harvard University Press, 2004.

Eberl, Jason T., and Kevin S. Decker eds. *Star Trek and Philosophy: The Wrath of Kant*. Chicago: Open Court, 1992.

Ede, Siân. *Art and Science*. New York: I. B. Tauris, 2005.

Egan, Michael. *Barry Commoner and the Science of Survival: The Remaking of American Environmentalism*. Cambridge, MA: MIT Press, 2009.

Eldridge, Richard. *Beyond Representation: Philosophy and Poetic Imagination*. New York: Cambridge University Press, 2011.

Fields, A. Belden. *Trotskyism and Maoism: Theory and Practice in France and the United States*. New York: Praeger, 1988.

Firor, John, and Judith Jacobsen. *The Crowded Greenhouse: Population, Climate Change, and Creating a Sustainable World*. New Haven: Yale University Press, 2002.

Frank, Adam. "Is a Climate Disaster Inevitable?" *New York Times*, January 18, 2015, SR6.

Frankfurt, Harry G. *The Reasons of Love*. Princeton, NJ: Princeton University Press, 2006.

Frölich, Paul. *Rosa Luxemburg: Her Life and Work*. New York: Howard Fertig, 1969.

Gallagher, Kelly Sims. *China Shifts Gears: Automakers, Oil, Pollution, and Development*. Cambridge, MA: MIT Press, 2006.

Gallagher, Mary Elizabeth. *Contagious Capitalism: Globalization and the Politics of Labor in China*. Princeton: Princeton University Press, 2005.

Gardner, Lloyd C. *Killing Machine: The American Presidency in the Age of Drone Warfare*. New York: New Press, 2013.

Gillis, Justin. "Ending Its Summer Melt, Arctic Sea Ice Sets a New Low That Leads to Warnings," *New York Times*, September 20, 2012, A8.

Gillis, Justin, and John M. Broder, "With Carbon Dioxide Emissions at Record High, Worries on How to Slow Warming," *New York Times*, December 3, 2012, A6.

Giroux, Henry A. *Zombie Politics and Culture in the Age of Casino Capitalism.* New York: Peter Lang, 2010.

Glock, Hans-Johann. *What is Analytic Philosophy?* New York: Cambridge University Press, 2008.

Gonzalez, George A. *Energy and the Politics of the North Atlantic.* Albany: State University of New York Press, 2013.

Gonzalez, George A. *The Politics of Star Trek: Justice, War, and the Future.* New York: Palgrave Macmillan, 2015.

Gonzalez, George A. *American Empire and the Canadian Oil Sands.* New York: Palgrave MacMillan, 2016a.

Gonzalez, George A. "*Justice League Unlimited* and the Politics of Globalization." *Foundation: The International Review of Science Fiction* 45, no. 123 (2016b): 5–13.

Goodman, Peter S. " U.S. and Global Economies Slipping in Unison," *New York Times,* August 24, 2008, A1.

Gordon, Paul. *Art as the Absolute: Art's Relation to Metaphysics in Kant, Fichte, Schelling, Hegel, and Schopenhauer.* New York: Bloomsbury Academic, 2015.

Gosetti-Ferencei, Jennifer Anna. *Heidegger, Holderlin, and the Subject of Poetic Language: Toward a New Poetics of Dasein.* New York: Forham University Press, 2009.

Greven, David. *Gender and Sexuality in Star Trek: Allegories of Desire in the Television Series and Films.* Jefferson: MacFarland, 2009.

Gross, Neil. *Richard Rorty: The Making of an American Philosopher.* Chicago: University of Chicago Press, 2008.

Hall, Martin, and Patrick Thaddeus Jackson, eds. *Civilization Identity.* New York: Palgrave Macmillan, 2007.

Hanley, Richard. *The Metaphysics of Star Trek.* New York: Basic, 1997.

Hark, Ina Rae. "Star Trek and Television's Moral Universe." *Extrapolation* 20, no. 1 (spring 1979): 20–37.

Harman, Chris. *Zombie Capitalism: Global Crisis and the Relevance of Marx.* Chicago: Haymarket Books, 2010.

Harrison, K. David. *When Languages Die: The Extinction of the World's Languages and the Erosion of Human Knowledge.* New York: Oxford University Press, 2008.

Harrison, Taylor, Sarah Projansky, Kent Ono, and Elyce Rae Helford, eds. *Enterprise Zones: Critical Positions on Star Trek.* Boulder: Westview, 1996.

Harvey, David. *Seventeen Contradictions and the End of Capitalism.* New York: Oxford University Press, 2014.

Haugeland, John. *Dasein Disclosed: John Haugeland's Heidegger.* Joseph Rouse, ed. Cambridge, MA: Harvard University Press, 2013.

Heidegger, Martin. *Being and Time.* New York: Harper Perennial Modern Classics, 2008 [1927].

Herf, Jeffrey. *The Jewish Enemy: Nazi Propaganda during World War II and the Holocaust.* Cambridge, MA: Harvard University Press, 2008.

Hickman, Larry A. *Pragmatism as Post-Modernism: Lessons from John Dewey.* New York: Forham University Press, 2007.

Hoff, Joan. *A Faustian Foreign Policy: From Woodrow Wilson to George W. Bush.* New York: Cambridge University Press, 2008.

Hoffman, Piotr. "Death, Time, History: Division II of *Being and Time.*" In *The Cambridge Companion to Heidegger,* ed. Charles B. Guigon. New York: Cambridge University Press, 2006.

Hook, Sidney. *Towards the Understanding of Karl Marx.* New York: John Day, 1933.

Horkheimer, Max. *Critique of Instrumental Reason* (trans: Matthew O'Connell). New York: Verso, 2013.

Houlgate, Stephen. *Hegel's 'Phenomenology of Spirit': A Reader's Guide.* New York: Bloomsbury Academic, 2013.

Hunt, Michael H. *The American Ascendancy: How the United States Gained and Wielded Global Dominance.* Chapel Hill: University of North Carolina Press, 2007.

Huntington, Samuel P. *The Clash of Civilizations and the Remaking of World Order.* New York: Simon & Schuster, 1996.

Hurdle, Jon. "Philadelphia Forges Plan To Rebuild From Decay," *New York Times,* January 1, 2014, B1.

Inayatullah, Naeem. "Bumpy Space: Imperialism and Resistance in *Star Trek: The Next Generation.*" In *To Seek Out New Worlds: Science Fiction and World Politics,* ed. Jutta Weldes. New York: Palgrave Macmillan, 2003.

Inwood, Michael. *Heidegger: A Very Short Introduction.* New York: Oxford University Press, 2000.

Johnson, Daryl, and Mark Potok. *Right-Wing Resurgence: How a Domestic Terrorist Threat is Being Ignored.* Lanham: Rowman & Littlefield, 2012.

Jones, Daniel Stedman. *Masters of the Universe: Hayek, Friedman, and the Birth of Neoliberal Politics.* Princeton: Princeton University Press, 2012.

Jones, Gareth Stedman. *Karl Marx: Greatness and Illusion.* Cambridge, MA: Harvard University Press, 2016.

Kaminsky, Jack. *Hegel on Art: An Interpretation of Hegel's Aesthetics.* Albany: State University of New York Press, 1962.

Kang, Cecilia. "New Robots in the Workplace: Job Creators or Job Terminators?" *Washington Post,* March 6, 2013. Web.

Kant, Immanuel. *Critique of Pure Reason* (trans: Max Muller). New York: Penguin, 2008 [1781].

Kemp, Martin. *Seen |Unseen: Art, Science, and Intuition from Leonardo to the Hubble Telescope.* New York: Oxford University Press, 2006.

Kershaw, Ian. *Hitler, the Germans, and the Final Solution.* New Haven: Yale University Press, 2009.

Kershaw, Ian. *Hitler: A Biography*. New York: Norton, 2010.

Kett, Joseph F. *Merit: The History of a Founding Ideal From the American Revolution to the Twenty-First Century*. Ithaca: Cornell University Press, 2013.

Kinney, Rebecca J. *Beautiful Wasteland: The Rise of Detroit as America's Postindustrial Frontier*. Minneapolis: University of Minnesota Press, 2016.

Klein, Gérard. "From the Images of Science to Science Fiction," In Learning from Other Worlds, ed. Patrick Parrinder. Durham: Duke University Press, 2001.

Klotzko, Arlene Judith. *A Clone of Your Own?* New York: Cambridge University Press, 2006.

Koistinen, David. *Confronting Decline: The Political Economy of Deindustrialization in Twentieth-Century New England*. Gainesville: University Press of Florida, 2013.

Kolbert, Elizabeth. *The Sixth Extinction: An Unnatural History*. New York: Henry Holt, 2014.

Kreines, James. *Reason in the World: Hegel's Metaphysics and Its Philosophical Appeal*. New York: Oxford University Press, 2015.

Krugman, Paul. "Robots and Robber Barons," *New York Times*, December 10, 2012, A27.

Kubálková, Vendulka, and Albert A. Cruickshank. *Marxism and International Relations*. New York: Oxford University Press, 1989.

Lacorne, Denis. *Religion in America: A Political History*. New York: Columbia University Press, 2001.

Lagon, Mark P. "'We Owe It to Them to Interfere:' *Star Trek* and U.S. Statecraft in the 1960s and the 1990s." In *Political Science Fiction*, eds Donald M. Hassler and Clyde Wilcox. Columbia: University of South Carolina Press, 1997.

Lenin, V.I. *Imperialism: The Highest Stage of Capitalism*. New York: Pluto, 1996 [1917].

Levine, Lawrence. *Highbrow/Lowbrow: The Emergence of Cultural Hierarchy in America*. Cambridge, MA: Harvard University Press, 1990.

Levick, Stephen E. *Clone Being: Exploring the Psychological and Social Dimensions*. Lanham, MD: Rowman & Littlefield, 2003.

MacFarquhar, Neil. "Russia, Jailer of Local Separatists, Hosts Foreign Ones." *New York Times*, September 26, 2016, A6.

MacGregor, David. *Hegel and Marx After the Fall of Communism*. Cardiff: University of Wales Press, [1998] 2014.

MacGregor, David. *The Communist Ideal in Hegel and Marx*. New York: Routledge, 2016.

Maker, William, ed. *Hegel and Aesthetics*. Albany: State University of New York Press, 2000.

Malabou, Catherine. *The Future of Hegel: Plasticity, Temporality and Dialectic*. New York: Routledge, 2004.

Malachowski, Alan. *The New Pragmatism*. Montreal: McGill-Queen's University Press, 2010.

Manjoo, Farhad. "Uber's Business Model Could Change Your Work," *New York Times*, January 29, 2015, B1.

Marx, Karl. *On the Jewish Question*, 1844: http://www.marxists.org/archive/marx/works/1844/jewish-question/.

Marx, Karl. *Critique of the Gotha Programme*. London: Electric Book Co., 2001 [1875].

Maslin, Mark. *Global Warming: A Very Short Introduction*. New York: Oxford University Press, 2009.

McCumber, John. *The Company of Words: Hegel, Language, and Systematic Philosophy*. Chicago: Northwestern University, 1993.

McCumber, John. *Time in a Ditch: American Philosophy in the McCarthy Era*. Evanston: Northwestern University Press, 2001.

McCumber, John. *Time and Philosophy: A History of Continental Thought*. Montreal: McGill-Queen's University Press, 2011.

McCumber, John. *The Philosophy Scare: The Politics of Reason in the Early Cold War*. Chicago: University of Chicago Press, 2016.

McGilvray, James. *Chomsky: Language, Mind, and Politics*. Cambridge: Polity, 1999.

McKee, Guin A. *The Problem of Jobs: Liberalism, Race, and Deindustrialization in Philadelphia*. Chicago: University of Chicago Press, 2009.

McLaren, Darcee L., and Jennifer E. Porter. "(Re) Covering Sacred Ground: New Age Spirituality in Star Trek: *Voyager*." In *Star Trek and Sacred Ground: Explorations of Star Trek, Religion, and American Culture*, ed. Jennifer E. Porter and Darcee L. McLaren. Albany: State University of New York Press, 1999.

McPherson, James M. *Abraham Lincoln and the Second American Revolution*. New York: Oxford University Press, 1992.

McPherson, James M. *Battle Cry of Freedom: The Civil War Era*. New York: Oxford University Press, 2003.

McWhorter, John H. *The Language Hoax: Why the World Looks the Same in Any Language*. New York: Oxford University Press, 2014.

Menand, Louis. *The Metaphysical Club*. New York: Farrar, Straus, and Giroux, 2001.

Miller, Carol Poh, and Robert Wheeler. *Cleveland: A Concise History*. Bloomington: Indiana University Press, 2009.

Miller, Claire Cain. "Smarter Robots Move Deeper Into Workplace," *New York Times*, December 16, 2014, A1.

Mozower, Mark. *Governing the World: The History of an Idea*. New York: Penguin Press, 2012.

Mumford, Stephen. *Metaphysics: A Very Short Introduction*. New York: Oxford University Press, 2012.

Myers, Constance Ashton. *The Prophet's Army: Trotskyists in America, 1928–1941.* Westport: Greenwood Press, 1977.

Nanay, Bence. *Aesthetics as Philosophy of Perception.* New York: Oxford University Press, 2016.

Nelson, Craig. *Thomas Paine: Enlightenment, Revolution, and the Birth of Modern Nations.* New York: Penguin, 2007.

Nexon, Daniel H., and Iver B. Neuman. *Harry Potter and International Relations.* Lanham: Rowman & Littlefield, 2006.

Nietzsche, Friedrich. *Beyond Good & Evil: Prelude to a Philosophy of the Future.* New York: Vintage, 1989 [1886].

O'Neill, Jere Surber, ed. *Hegel and Language.* Albany: State University of New York Press, 2006.

Oakes, James. *Freedom National: The Destruction of Slavery in the United States.* New York: W.W. Norton & Company, 2012.

Osborne, Peter. *The Politics of Time: Modernity and Avant-Garde.* New York: Verso, 1995.

Padgett, Deborah K., Benjamin F. Henwood, and Sam J. Tsemberis. *Housing First: Ending Homelessness, Transforming Systems, and Changing Lives.* New York: Oxford University Press, 2015.

Palmer, Bryan D. *James P. Cannon and the Origins of the American Revolutionary Left, 1890–1928.* Urbana: University of Illinois Press, 2010.

Paolucci, Henry. "Introduction." In *Hegel: On the Arts*, ed. Henry Paolucci (2nd edn.). Smyrna: Griffon House, 2001.

Parr, Adrian. *The Wrath of Capital: Neoliberalism and Climate Change Politics.* New York: Columbia University Press, 2013.

Pearson, Anne Mackenzie. "From Thwarted Gods to Reclaimed Mystery?: An Overview of the Depiction of Religion in *Star Trek.*" In *Star Trek and Sacred Ground: Explorations of Star Trek, Religion, and American Culture*, ed. Jennifer E. Porter and Darcee L. McLaren. Albany: State University of New York Press, 1999.

Perkins, Robert L., ed. *History and System: Hegel's Philosophy of History.* Albany: State University of New York, 1984.

Pillow, Kirk. *Sublime Understanding: Aesthetic Reflection in Kant and Hegel.* Cambridge, MA: MIT Press, 2000.

Polk, Sam. "For the Love of Money," *New York Times*, January 19, 2014, SR1.

Powell, James Lawrence. *The Inquisition of Climate Science.* New York: Columbia University Press, 2011.

Rauchway, Eric. *The Great Depression and the New Deal: A Very Short Introduction.* New York: Oxford University Press, 2008.

Read, Christopher. *Lenin: A Revolutionary Life.* New York: Routledge, 2005.

Richards, Thomas. *The Meaning of Star Trek.* New York: Doubleday, 1997.

Roberts, Robin. *Sexual Generations: "Star Trek: The Next Generation" and Gender.* Chicago: University of Illinois Press, 1999.

Robertson, Thomas. *The Malthusian Moment: Global Population Growth and the Birth of American Environmentalism.* New Brunswick: Rutgers University Press, 2012.

Romano, Carlin. *America the Philosophical.* New York: Simon & Schuster, 2012.

Rorty, Richard. *Philosophy and the Mirror of Nature.* Princeton: Princeton University Press, 1981.

Rubin, Derek, and Jaap Verheul, eds. *American Multiculturalism after 9/11: Transatlantic Perspectives.* Amsterdam: Amsterdam University Press, 2010.

Sabin, Paul. *The Bet: Paul Ehrlich, Julian, and Our Gamble over Earth's Future.* New Haven: Yale University Press, 2013.

Sandel, Adam Adatto. *The Place of Prejudice: A Case for Reasoning in the World.* Cambridge, MA: Harvard University Press, 2014.

Schecter, Darrow. *The Critique of Instrumental Reason from Weber to Habermas.* New York: Bloomsbury Academic, 2012.

Schlesinger, Arthur M. *The Disuniting of America: Reflections on a Multicultural Society.* New York: W.W. Norton, 1988.

Schmitt, Carl. *The Concept of the Political.* expanded edition. Chicago: University of Chicago University, 2007 [1929].

Schwartz, Stephen P. *A Brief History of Analytic Philosophy: From Russell to Rawls.* Hoboken: Wiley-Blackwell, 2012.

Seefeldt, Kristin S., and John D. Graham. *America's Poor and the Great Recession.* Bloomington: Indiana University Press, 2013.

Shanker, Thom. "Simple, Low-Cost Drones a Boost for U.S. Military," *New York Times,* January 25, 2013, A12.

Shapiro, Alan. *Star Trek. Technologies of Disappearance.* Berlin: Avinus Press, 2004.

Singer, Irving. *Philosophy of Love: A Partial Summing-Up.* Cambridge, MA: MIT Press, 2011.

Singer, Peter. *Hegel: A Very Short Introduction.* New York: Oxford University Press, 2001a.

Singer, Peter. *Marx: A Very Short Introduction.* New York: Oxford University Press, 2001b.

Smith, Eric D. *Globalization, Utopia, and Postcolonial Science Fiction.* New York: Palgrave Macmillan, 2012.

Smith, Neil. *Uneven Development: Nature, Capital, and the Production of Space* (3rd edn.). Athens: University of Georgia Press, 2008.

Solnit, Rebecca. "Bird by Bird," *New York Times Magazine,* December 7, 2014, MM13.

Stack, Liam. "Globalism: A Far-Right Conspiracy Theory Buoyed by Trump." *New York Times,* November 14, 2016. Web.

Stern, David S., ed. *Essays on Hegel's Philosophy of Subjective Spirit.* Albany: State University of New York Press, 2013.

Sugrue, Thomas J. *The Origins of the Urban Crisis: Race and Inequality in Postwar Detroit.* Princeton: Princeton University Press, 2005.

"Ten States Still Have Fewer Jobs Since Recession," *Reuters,* March 25, 2016.

Trotsky, Leon. *History of the Russian Revolution.* New York: Pathfinder, 1980 [1933].

Tufekci, Zeynep. "The Machines Are Coming," *New York Times,* April 19, 2015, SR4.

Uchitelle, Louis. "Goodbye, Production (and Maybe Innovation)." *New York Times,* December 24, 2006, sec. 3 p. 4.

Unger, Harlow Giles. *Lafayette.* Hoboken: Wiley, 2003.

Uscinski, Joseph E., and Joseph M. Parent. *American Conspiracy Theories.* New York: Oxford University Press, 2014.

Vegso, Roland. *The Naked Communist: Cold War Modernism and the Politics of Popular Culture.* New York: Fordham University Press, 2013.

Verene, Donald Phillip. *Hegel's Absolute: An Introduction to Reading the Phenomenology of Spirit.* Albany: State University New York Press, 2007.

Vernon, Jim. *Hegel's Philosophy of Language.* London: Continuum, 2007.

Wachter, Susan M., and Kimberly A. Zeuli, eds. *Revitalizing American Cities.* Philadelphia: University of Pennsylvania Press, 2013.

Wade, Nicholas. "Scientists Seek Ban on Method of Editing the Human Genome," *New York Times,* March 20, 2015, A1.

Wagner, Jon, and Jan Lundeen. *Deep Space and Sacred Time: Star Trek in the American Mythos.* Westport: Praeger, 1998.

Walsh, Declan, and Ihsanullan Tipu Mehsud, "Civilian Deaths in Drone Strikes Cited in Report," *New York Times,* October 22, 2013, A1.

Walzer, Michael. *Thinking Politically: Essays in Political Theory.* ed. David Miller. New Haven: Yale University Press, 2007.

Weisberg, Josh. *Consciousness.* Cambridge, MA: Polity, 2014.

Westerhoff, Jan. *Reality: A Very Short Introduction.* New York: Oxford University Press, 2012.

Williams, Timothy. "For Shrinking Cities, Destruction Is a Path to Renewal," *New York Times,* November 12, 2013, A15.

Willse, Craig. *The Value of Homelessness: Managing Surplus Life in the United States.* Minneapolis: University of Minnesota Press, 2015.

Worland, Rick. "Captain Kirk: Cold Warrior." *Journal of Popular Film & Television* 16, no. 3 (1988): 109–117.

Zuckert, Michael P., and Catherine H. Zuckert. *Leo Strauss and the Problem of Political Philosophy.* Chicago: University of Chicago Press, 2014.

INDEX

© The Author(s) 2017
G.A. Gonzalez, *The Absolute and Star Trek*,
DOI 10.1007/978-3-319-47794-7

113